I Throw Like a Girl

"Chuck Forester's memoir is testament to a life fully embraced and lived out loud—sexy, ribald, elegiac, and proud. A gay elder looks back at lost histories and making a difference—essential lessons for all of us in the queer community." —John Killacky, former legislator, artist, and arts administrator

"Chuck's writing transports me to a San Francisco that I get the chance to go back in time to through his fresh and detailed experiences. It's refreshing to read about gay sex in such a candid narrative and I'm sure other readers will feel the same way. Chucks memoir is part of the queer nonfiction canon and memorializes those who died tragically of AIDS with dignity, grace and unabashed honesty." —Grace Jordan, playwright

"Chuck Forester was in part of the queer generation just before mine, and one of my go-to insider sources for San Francisco's gay history in the '70s, back when I was learning my way around town. His memoir is a welcome, inspiring blast from the past about those halcyon days." —Susan Stryker, co-author, *Gay by the Bay: A History of Queer San Francisco*

"There are all sorts of recollections of the riotous, libidinous, bold, brazen gay life that manifested during the shining sliver of opportunity that occurred between the Stonewall Riot and the first crushing tidal bore of AIDS deaths—but few of them are as unapologetic, candid, and self-revealing as this one. And because Chuck Forester has been fortunate enough to wrestle HIV to a draw over the past four decades, he is here to tell us what it has been like to live on, to remember the joy and jubilation, to bear witness, to burnish our collective legacy." —Ned Bayrd, author

"Loving your book, and so appreciate the *Fisting for Dummies* section—that is a great contribution to gay letters." —Trebor Healey, author of *Falling*

"As a fellow queer Wisconsinite who moved to San Francisco in the disco '70s, I applaud the author for his resolute memories and assessments. From his pronouncements of the stone, gothic mansions on Lake Drive in Milwaukee to our glory holes on South of Market, no relevant detail is ignored or dismissed. Passionate and true, do read this book." —Mark Leno, former Democratic member of the California State Senate

I Throw Like a Girl

ALSO BY CHUCK FORESTER

I Throw Like a Girl

Eat, Sleep, Love

Our Time

I Throw Like a Girl
a memoir

Chuck Forester

Querelle Books
New York, NY

I Throw Like a Girl: A Memoir
Copyright © 2022 by Chuck Forester

Cover design by Paul Chamberlain, Cerebral Itch.

Book cover image used with permission from the GLBT Historical Society.

Published by Querelle Press, LLC
2808 Broadway, #15
New York, NY 10025
www.querellepress.com

ISBN 979-8-9850341-2-7, paper edition
ISBN 979-8-9850341-3-4, e-book edition

Distributed by Ingram Content Group
To order: Ingramcontent.com

Printed in the United States
First US Edition

for

Seth and Michael

Acknowledgments

I think nothing of kissing a man and saying I slept with him.

In 1972, the only place I could do that was San Francisco.

Most of the men who made that possible are gone. AIDS took the life-affirming men who gave me that freedom, but they cannot disappear.

I acknowledge them here.

It takes a family to write a book. My family includes a fine editor, Don Weise, Ned Bayrd, Jeff Bosacki, Jewelle Gomez, David Groff, Trebor Healey, William Johnson, Grace Jordan, John Killacky, Mark Leno, Michael Nava, Richard Street, Susan Stryker, and Tim Wolfred. With special thanks to Michael Samuel.

Contents

Let's Get Started

The year is 1972, the year I came out. A disowned fourteen-year-old gay boy in Shaker Heights is left on the street, a principal tells a teenage lesbian in Minneapolis if she wants to graduate, she must wear a skirt, and a young Black boy in Jacksonville, hears the pastor demonize boys like him as work of the devil. 1972 was hard on queer people.

I came out at twenty-eight in San Francisco, and I jumped into the rainbow as part of the Great Migration; thousands of queer men and women who moved to the only city in America where we could hold hands in public. A hefty injection of hippie free love freed me to be me and using what I learned from the men I had sex with, I fashioned a fully functioning faggot. Because it's the easiest way for me to make friends, I had sex with them first.

There were no gay role models in Wausau, Wisconsin

because gay men in 1972 were in their closets clutching their Martinis and hoping Tallulah Bankhead would rescue them. The rich cultural ferment of San Francisco produced perfect role models for the times. Jack Garcia taught me the art of cruising and inviting a man home for sex. Clay Grillo showed me his California's wilderness and how to accept pleasure when a man has his dick inside me. Bill Day and Jim Hickey's rock-solid relationship epitomized love. There were no better models of honest gay love.

Love in Wausau was transactional because I measured Dad's caring by the value of his Christmas presents. My boyfriend Michael A. Schoch changed that. He gave me the most profound gift a man can give a man: eighteen years of unconditional love. My playing around scared off lesser men, but he stayed true to me, something that continues to amaze me. He went to the Glorious Bathhouse in the Sky in 1994, but whenever I'm in the kitchen, his spirit rummages around inside of me.

I was the first out gay man in San Francisco's mayor's office and knowing that Harvard law grad Al Baum was out at the Bay Conservation and Development Commission told me I was in good company. He and Jim Hormel, heir to the Hormel Meat fortune both generous philanthropists loved me, and they made me a smart philanthropist.

Al was in his element when he made it to three different queer fundraising dinners in a single evening on his red Vespa. His enthusiasm for the community energized me. Jim asked me to replace him on the board of the fledgling Human Rights Campaign Fund, and I swelled with pride every time he showed up the worst of America. He was the understanding father I never had.

I followed their path as I rose through the ranks at the Human Rights Campaign Fund in the eighties, now the Human Rights Campaign, the most politically powerful queer organization in the country, and later when I raised $3.5 million for the Hormel Gay and Lesbian Center in The San Francisco Public Library.

HIV was onboard by 1978 or earlier because my blood was frozen as part of a Hep C study in 1978. Once it could be tested, Michael checked on his blood, and he was positive. We enjoyed six incredible years of roll around joyous unprotected sex, so if he was positive, I was positive.

I have a powerful immune system that has allowed me to live the greatest times a gay man could ever live, the early '70s in San Francisco, when we taught each other what it means to be a gay man as we created gay Mecca in the Castro. It was there again in the '80s when the loss of thousands of honorable men to AIDS made us a political force to be reckoned with.

I have only so much time on this planet, so I write this story so my son will have something when his grandchildren ask about his gay dad.

Sex was a big part of my life, so I include it here in all its lurid detail.

If you are hesitant around sex, give it a second look. Sex is lots of fun when it's done right. And don't be embarrassed if it doesn't work the first time. That's natural. Sex is better the second time, and the more sex you have the better you get.

WAUSAU

Wausau, Wisconsin

Wausau, Wisconsin, once the timber capital of the country, was a mill town of beer and brawlers. When I got to Wausau in 1948, the days of the timber barons was waning, but it was still a timber town. My wealthy is the result of one of the timber barons making a fortune.

Walter Alexander and Cyrus Yawkey made fortunes at the turn of the last century by turning centuries old stands of white pine in northern Wisconsin into timber.

When I got to town, the chamber of commerce displayed a six feet wide slice of a white pine in front of the Richardson-style county courthouse. Our high school mascot was a lumberjack. My second home was the home of Walter Alexander's sister.

My family's fortunes depended on the fortune of Cyrus Yawkey's because I came to Wausau in 1948, so Dad could take a job with Atchymonde Woodson. He was married to

Leigh Yawkey, and she was the sole heir to her father Cyrus Yawkey's timber fortune. I was involved more than I wanted with the Yawkey Woodson family until Dad died.

I had a family and then it was taken away. My first family was a typical of Midwest families in the Fifties. Dad went to work at eight. He walked home at noon bringing with him a loaf of white bread from the Community Bake Shop. He walked home again at five. We ate dinner at five-thirty, so he could watch Douglas Edwards and the news, and we could only talk during commercials. That was the only time the family was in the same room.

Mom was the traditional housewife. She kept our home and her three sons clothing clean, plus she prepared three meals a day for the family.

Older brother John went out for junior high football. He modeled himself after Dad.

I was the middle son, I liked learning and watching Mom prepare meals. I learned to play the piano using chords.

Younger brother Rick had emotional problems and spent most of his time in his room.

When I was in eighth grade my family was taken from me. Dad started an affair with his boss's daughter Alice Woodson Hagge, so he left the house at seven. She had more money and better real estate, so from then on it was always her game. He wanted to spend as much time as possible with her, and he came up with a string of excuses. It started with "Watching Sunday football at her house is better because her sunroom holds more people." It went from there to my entire family spending the summer at Point O Pines, the estate her grandfather built as his summer residence on a lake up north, with Dad and her husband Robert commuting to Wausau. That didn't work very long because is the great drama called life, it tested their patience, and the man whose wife is seeing another man doesn't like being around the man who stole his wife. That hiccup didn't stop Dad from having me spend my summers at Point O Pines until I left for college.

Point O Pines had everything a kid desires, a Criss Craft, a ski boat, a trampoline and two-level raft and water skiing every day. Nice as it was, it was a gilded cage removed from the real world, and it operated on her terms that were built around isolation.

Aside from the Yawkey Woodson wealth and properties, there was nothing there. Beneath the gilt of wealth, the Woodson family was emotionally dead. Like most wealthy couples, Mr. and Ms. Woodson had no interest in being parents, a chore they left to others. First born, Cyrus Woodson, a wealthy playboy had zero interest in following in his father's footsteps. At twenty-one, he put a bullet through his head Christmas Day. To preserve his memory, his mother kept his room exactly the way it was the day he died, and she wouldn't let anyone touch it until she moved many years later. The Woodsons left the raising of their remaining three daughters to a young woman they imported from France. Think how creepy it would be to grow up in a home with dead person preserved in his bedroom.

Oldest daughter Nancy Leigh Woodson was scary. She wore dark glasses during the day inside, so she was an ominous presence. As soon as she could away from her family, she married a doctor and moved to Fayetteville, New York. Youngest daughter Margaret Woodson, the athlete and smoker, was afraid to fly, but as soon as she could get away from her family, she married a doctor and took the train to Fort. Lauderdale, Florida, where she built a home so large it became an attraction on tourist canal boat tours.

Middle daughter Alice Woodson stayed in Wausau, and she along with Dad destroyed my family. Like it or not, she was the dominant fixture in my life until I left for college.

My family didn't do much better when it came to emotions. Dad came from a Methodist family in Wauwatosa that didn't read the Sunday paper on Sunday because Sunday was a day of reflection. His mother, wound tight as a drum, was a tyrant for cleanliness, and she didn't let him get out of the house until he'd done his chores to her exacting standards. If she ran her finger across the top of a bureau and found dust, he had to clean it as many times as it took for her to run her finger across the bureau and find no dust. Dad had no love because he got none from her. He believed children should be obedient.

Dad had the same haircut he had as boy the day he died. His routines never varied. He wore the same dark blue suit and a rep striped tie every day for thirty years.

He was a life-long Republican who served as an FBI agent during the Second World War. Those values got passed on to me, so in 1952 at age eight, because I was supposed to be a Republican, I argued with my best friend David Schilling for the re-election of that piece of shit Senator Joseph McCarthy.

Dad asked me what I wanted to be when I was an adult. I told him I wanted to be happy. He scoffed at that. "Happiness is working hard so you can earn enough money to support your family."

His obsession with wealth complicated things further. At a time when I needed emotional support, the only support he could give me was financial.

He insisted on being right, so I gave up on engaging him in conversation.

I lived my way, and rather than trying to understand me, Dad turned discipline over to Mom.

He insisted I be an attorney; I insisted on being me.

Mom was the daughter of a prominent Milwaukee attorney. She grew up on North Shepherd Avenue on Milwaukee's fashionable East Side. She was a fun and games girl who dated Augie Pabst of the Pabst brewing family. In Madison, her mother's sorority taught her that a good wife is subservient to her husband.

She had little interest in politics, but with a Republican US Senator in her family, she followed the family tradition and automatically voted Republican.

She wore beige, but she let me do what I wanted to do.

One day, she told me Peter Schuler's mother told her I touched her son's Peter's peter. Of course, I did, but I denied it vigorously. She gave me the absolute best advice a mom can give her gay son, "Don't get caught."

When a babysitter saw me in one of Mom's dresses, she took a picture. Mom framed the photo and kept it on top of the piano where it taunted me until I left for college.

I got my love of words from her. The first book she read to me was Alice's Adventures in Wonderland. She loved taking me down the Jabberwocky poem, purposely mispronouncing the names of the characters to make me laugh. We competed at punning, the more outrageous the pun the better. She was the only person in my family to attend my theatrical performances. When I was in college, she was still correcting my grammar.

She was conflict averse with the marvelous ability to start every day fresh. With all the shit of yesterday gone, every day began with a clean slate. She listened to my complaints about John picking on me but never did anything about it. Her aversion to conflict kept her from raising a stink over Dad's affair with Alice. I never saw her cry. I got my brain from her, so she knew Dad was never coming back, but it was crunch time, so she retreated to avoid conflict. She abhorred pity, but it was her steadfast love of Dad that kept a situation that involved two wealthy people who had no control over their emotions from flying spectacularly off the rails. To paraphrase *Go High on that Mountain.* "Mom, I know your life was troubled, and only you can know your pain. Go rest easy in your bedroom on North Shepard Avenue."

Alice's husband, Robert Hagge, wanted to spend his evenings with Mom. He was born to wealth and never grew up, but he loved his four kids. His drinking problem crashed two cars. He needed someone to care for him and his need set off Mom's need to take care of someone.

There was no happiness in the Forester home because Dad got none growing up. Winter nine months of the year kills healthy spirits, and my memories of winter are shoveling snow and freezing my ass off in the back of Alice's DeSoto station wagon as I am dragged to a miserable ski hill. Each time, I'm told to ski with her four kids all younger while John gets to ski with the adults.

By the time I was in eighth grade, I was on my own. When John left for college, and I got the servant's quarters. I was fifty feet from the main house. The sitting room had a TV, and I ran campaigns for friends who were running for student council president there. It is also the site of a boy slumber party. Ronny Yonke and I slept over at each other's homes where we touched and mutually masturbated. He was an alcoholic, and the bathroom has handy when I had to clean him up so he could go home.

I kept a large jar of Vaseline and a box of Kleenex on the bedside table in my bedroom along with my abused copy of *Physique Pictoral* with men in posing straps. I jacked off every day, often three or four times. When Mom asked about the Vaseline, I explained that I used the Vaseline on the flat top that I didn't have.

One room was my sanctuary, and my correcting electric typewriter had pride of place on an old wooden desk. One wall had a window, so in the winter, I looked at frozen blackness. The opposite wall had a giant gold framed painting of a Roman chariot race with teams of snorting horses that once hung in the Yawkey home. Trapped between the blackness and the snorting horses, I set up my command center. I sent a letter every week about LRY, the youth organization of the Unitarian Universalist Church, to my friends who lived in the Twin Cities. I sent a four-page letter every week to Debby Snow in Saint Petersburg, Florida. I asked her the civil rights struggle in the South, and I shared my dreams of alleviating poverty. I never said anything to any of them about my family because they embarrassed me.

In my first year at Dartmouth, Ms. Woodson died. With her gone, Alice could now divorce Robert and Dad followed suit divorcing Mom. A year later, according to Wisconsin law that made them wait a year, Dad married Alice, and Mom married Robert. My uncomfortable pretend family was now two families. I didn't like either of them, but as the dutiful son who was counting on his inheritance, I made Christmas visits until Mom died.

Wife swapping and a wealthy family was the recipe for gossip of *Dallas* proportions. It should have been snatched by every editor in the Midwest, but Alice and Dad never made the news because they were tight with Mac McCormick, the publisher of the *Wausau Daily Herald*. It's good to be the king.

Payback for Dad's miserliness was his promise that there

would be something for me when he died. Since there was nothing I could do about it, I accepted stuffing the loss of my family as trade for not struggling financially once he was gone. I'd gone through a lot of lies but by then, so I knew the game, and I could suffer more grief until he died.

Liz Seidel, a Lutheran pastor's daughter, saved my ass when my family was dissolving. We were named "wittiest" in the 1962 Wausau Senior High yearbook. Every year the yearbook used the same sets, best athlete, most favorite student, ad nauseum. I got kicked off the yearbook staff because I wanted my year's yearbook to look hipper.

She was my favorite dance partner at Teen Town, the Friday night dance at the YWCA, and she was my co-conspirator at school. We did a variety show in her garage using props from an eleven-minute PTA skit that Mom produced and directed.

One night, sitting around in the parsonage's dining room of heavy, dark furniture with a bowl of cold pasta, we couldn't stop laughing as we made fun of our teachers. Her take on our third-grade teacher was spot on. A favorite target was the clique of girls who decided who merited membership in their cult when cloistered in the girl's cloak room at Teen Town.

By end of the night, we were in stitches, and she'd eaten the bowl of pasta.

Liz is the reason I went to class reunions. At the second, instead of playing the great tunes of the fifties like the Everly brothers, a polka band reminded me Wausau is a working-class city with German and Polish roots.

She graduated from a Lutheran college, and she's been married to the same man since they got married. She lives in Minneapolis and has no children. We stay in touch via email, and she sends me birthday cards. She's kept my spirits up in dark times.

I can't be certain when my internal homophobia was implanted, but I know where it came from. The distrust of strangers was so pervasive among the clean, hardworking people of Wausau that I didn't need to hear the words. I knew from the way they reacted to Black people and the Japanese that they would despise men who had sex with men. Just the mention of men living together would have them calling the police. I got it from the slurs about queers in Scout camp. I got it watching TV, where effeminate characters were treated as jokes. I got it overhearing jocks making fun of queers in the locker room. I got it from Dad because I wasn't the son he wanted.

I got most of it from my older brother, John. From the time I was three, he abused me verbally and physically. He beat my shoulders and head like a mad man beating a drum until I was twelve. It was then I realized that if I didn't act hurt, he stopped beating me because then he wasn't getting the satisfaction he needed to show me that he was Dad's favorite. His verbal abuse continued.

His favorite on the Hit Parade of Pain was "You throw like a girl." By inference, he was saying I wasn't a man. I wasn't a man stuck, and it's the subtext of my life. It's hard to talk about not being a man because I don't want to appear to be weak. I've dealt with it over the years by working around it.

Point O' Pines was Alice's summer residence starting in 1950. In the 1960s, she and Dad tore down Cyrus Yawkey's Victorian, and they replaced it with a California-style home that they kept enlarging. Standing in the volleyball court, Leigh gave me a bag containing both Dad and Alice's ashes.

I resented scattering Dad's ashes mixed with Alice's because I was abetting Dad in his abandonment of his family for the last time. No kid should ever have to do that to his family.

The remains of my parents rest on property owned by my stepparents' families, a telling sign of my destroyed family. The Forester family leaves no trace in Wausau aside from Dad's name on the donor wall of the Leigh Yawkey Woodson Art Museum. It's ironic that the obituary for Dad online does not mention Alice, and I found no obituary for him in the *Wausau Daily Herald*.

Yawkey Woodson family secrets were meant to stay secret.

The Beat Goes On

I knew I couldn't be a good father, so I didn't want children. My life was lived in rejection from Dad, so I had nothing to build a good father on. My then-wife Christine came from a family of four children, and she wanted children.

We met on a trip to Europe that summer after I graduated from Dartmouth. When my affair in grad school wasn't going anywhere, I tried being straight and asked her to come to Philadelphia. While we were in Chile as Peace Corps volunteers, I kept putting off having a baby, and she told me she would stop taking the pill in August. That gave me some breathing room, but I still didn't want children because a child deserved a calm home and a caring father, and I couldn't do that.

My idea of being gay wasn't fully formed, but I remembered that first kiss in the lace curtain room in New Cannan, and the spark hadn't died, but I was resigned to being the parent because that's what my classmates at Penn were doing, but I wasn't happy about it because my future was bleak.

She stopped the pill in July, and Seth was conceived that month when we were in Rio de Janeiro on the month vacation the Peace Corps allowed us.

When we came back from the Peace Corps, we stayed temporarily with her parents in Winchester because her family kept the Irish Setter we sent ahead from Chile to Logan Airport. I bought a BMW 2002, and we drove it across country on the southern route because it was January.

Outside of Bakersfield, Seth was running a high temperature. I raced us to the nearest hospital, and I waited in a featureless waiting room while an ER nurse submerged Seth in an ice bath to cool him down. I was surprised at how maturely I handled it.

1971 was an early year for smog controls on cars, and I had the car in the shop twice to fix the controls. The costs of the German repairs with my meager savings were astronomical. I loved the car, but once Seth was born, Christine insisted we have a Volvo wagon. I learned early that it was better to give in to her than to argue with her because once her mind was set, there was no changing it. I wasn't happy, but hurting my pride by giving in was less onerous than hurting my pride by losing an argument because I was the one with the brains.

The evening I left the home in Berkeley that Dad helped me buy to live with Jack Garcia, the man who brought me out, I pulled away in his VW bug, and when I saw two-year-old Seth wave from the porch I broke down. I loved the little guy.

To legally end our marriage we used the same attorney. Christine was moderate in her demands for spousal support. She also gave me the greatest gift when I told her I wanted to explore my bisexuality. She knew about my affair in grad school and said, "Not in my house."

That set me free to begin my life as a gay man with no strings attached.

I had Seth every other weekend until he was eighteen.

On her own for the first time, Christine needed a college degree, and the reason she chose Mills College was because it meant Seth would be close to his father. I can't thank her enough for that.

Seth had a difficult childhood because Christine married a jerk, and he didn't like Seth because he wasn't his son. When he was young, his mother was busy starting a new marriage, so she neglected him. Coming to San Francisco every other week got him away from that. I was his safe retreat.

Like a good solider, Seth rode busses to be with me. Every other Friday, when Christine was getting a degree at Mills College he got on a bus in Oakland. Later when she was working for the state government, she put him on a bus in Sacramento.

He gets his reticence from me, so he doesn't like talking about his feelings about his mother or her husband. He was safe with me, and he did reveal some of his anger and resentment. He's remarkably sensible.

I wanted to engage Seth in the life of the city, but after seeing what happened to Alice's trust fund children who had everything, I didn't want him to think of me as Santa Claus. I grew up with lies, and I'd had it with pretending to be someone else. The best way I could be a father to Seth was to be me unvarnished.

Seth watched me live my everyday life as a gay man and that often meant me being stoned with friends as we created Gay Mecca. He sat with a pad and pencil drawing quietly. I told him "I love you" every day.

I indulged him with rides on the carousel in Golden Gate Park, performances of the Michael Smuin ballet, and art material and clothing every year at Christmas. Many of his meals were prepared by Michael, so he developed a taste for fine food. I took him to London for a week. He's an avid Anglophile, and he has a classic Mini Cooper.

The only time he saw me having sex was the day he saw me fucking Robert Scott. The first time I saw Robert was the day he dropped by the community development offices in the basement of City Hall. He was mixed-race Black, Cape Veridian and white. His beauty was stunning. I'd never seen anyone that beautiful. He rented the apartment across the hall from me on Diamond Street and we shared our lives for a few months. He was fiercely jealous and my fooling around was too much for him, so we split up. Our love continued. We stayed in touch with the occasional emails and him sending me vintage photos of gay men. He died of a brain disease. I miss his sly messages.

When Michael and I were in Europe, Seth stayed in our flat. There was a party, and someone slipped Seth LSD without telling him. That is the egregious crime. He had a horrific reaction that got physical, and he had to be restrained. He spent a night in hospital. That experience keeps him from doing drugs.

The year he was enrolled at State he lived in the bottom flat of my three Edwardian flat building on Fulton Street. He's not a good student; he needs space to create art, so he got a degree from the Academy of Art University.

He was with me when I met Michael for the first time at his cabin, and Seth spent many weekends at the cabin, giving him direct experience with California wilderness. One summer, Michael hired him to work as part of his landscaping crew. Seth saw Michael as a parent, and I wanted him to witness Michael's dying because Death is part of life, and unlike me who was sheltered, he should experience a broad spectrum of feelings.

Seth taught me to be a good father. He always looked up to me, and I relied on him when I made horrible mistakes like the time we were in Disneyland. My AIDS meds caused explosive diarrhea, so while I sheltered in Mickey Mouse's men's room in a puddle of the aftermath of the diarrhea and soiled paper towels stinking to high heaven, he bought me a new pair of shorts. I cleaned up in the sink.

After Michael died, he was concerned about me being happy. He saw me through three affairs always absorbing.

I've watched Seth as he made a life for himself, sure of his talents as an artist. He's gone through some rough times, but he's stayed true to himself. He is married to his soulmate, Cassandra, and I've never seen him happier.

I have a distant relationship with my granddaughter Taija. I knew my genes were passed on when she told me her sexuality is fluid. She recently graduated from Sacramento State and lives with her boyfriend in her mother's home in San Francisco. I see her every Christmas.

I thought after I separated from Christine that I'd be free of dealing with female energy that's a complete mystery to me because I grew up in a family of three boys and I went to an all-male college. Now with Cassandra, having a daughter takes some serious readjustments.

I worried Seth would be bulled when the kids in school found out he had a gay dad. He said, "They think it's cool my dad is gay. They want their own gay dad."

I did something right as a father.

Brother Rick's sexuality has evolved over time. He had an early fascination with Mom's lingerie. He thought about sex reassignment. He was a crossdresser and at least one of his wives knew about it, but I don't know how much she helped him. When he was as crossdresser, Michael took him to a Tenderloin bar where he met a transvestite, and they had a two-day dalliance.

He came into his own when he adopted the twin children of his second wife's daughter who abandoned them. Being a good and patient father was what he was put on this earth to do. His twins are now college age, and he is bisexual and living with a woman in North Carolina. He sends me queer things he finds on the Internet.

After graduating from law school in Madison, John stayed in Wausau, where he worked for the top law firm there. He lived until a few years ago in Saratoga Springs, New York, where he worked for another law firm. He's had a second home in Vail for years. He now lives in a retirement community in outside of Denver where he's close to his daughter, who is around Seth's age.

He's had three wives, and he's close to his daughter. He was a top-notch oldest brother when our parents died. He took care of legal work professionally, and both distributions went smoothly.

When I was fifty, John told me he'd been a poor brother, and I forgave him. A few years later, he said my life was more exciting than his life. That, for me, that was the sweetest revenge.

We aren't close but we do the brother thing well, and we communicate via email. He spent three days with me in Sebastopol, and he's been invaluable when I needed to know something of the timing of an event in Wausau for this memoir.

I returned to Wausau twice for the funerals of my parents.

After Mom married Robert, they built a house in Wausau with a swimming pool. Four years later, they enclosed it, using one of the early solar heating systems that needed constant adjustments. Her cholesterol story starts with her cocktail hour snacks of hard yellow cheese and dark sausage, sometimes venison. It gets serious when her dinner three nights of the week was a New York steak and a baked potato and butter.

Her doctor put her on blood pressure meds and told her to stop drinking hard liquor with dark colors. She took the meds and switched from her Jim Beam before dinner and another couple after dinner to a vodka soda before dinner and one after dinner and another when she felt she needed one.

After Robert died of a brain aneurism, she refused to do simple things like go for a walk or exercise that would keep her alive. She was destined to die like her mother, and she wasn't trying to stop it.

Dad cheated on her, and Robert was a marriage of convenience, but Norman Bearse, her third husband, was her decision, and he was her ticket to freedom. For the first time in her life, at sixty-nine, she could be herself and live happily with her man in a new home on the other side of town. It was a beautiful ride, but it didn't last long. She suffered two strokes, the second a month after the first one, left like her mother.

I sat with her for a week, and the only time she registered attention was the time Norman entered the room. She left explicit instructions that she did not want her life prolonged.

In the frenzy around her death at the hospital, I had to corral my brothers, several step siblings, and her sister, put them in a room and get them to agree to stop her life; younger brother Rick held out the longest. Assisted suicide was illegal in Wisconsin, but someone overheard a family member in another family talk about how they stopped feeding a parent who was in situation like Mom's. I instructed a nurse to stop feeding her, and she died of pneumonia four days later in 1988, age seventy-four.

I'll never know what was going on in her mind her last days, but I'd like to think she started each day fresh.

Mom seldom attended church, and so I suggested we do a memorial service, and no brother had a better idea. Memorial services were the way I remembered my friends who died of AIDS, but they hadn't made it as far as Wausau. The service was held in the Wausau Club, a private dining club founded by Mr. Yawkey and other lumber barons. City improvements like Yawkey Park and Stewart Park started in the club. The small group of Mom's friends who'd never seen a memorial service didn't know what to make of the service, so no one volunteered to say something about Mom when they were given the opportunity.

The service was a dud, but Mom was glad she missed it. She was never big on groups or being the center of attention.

Brother John very ably managed the reading of her will and the legal details of her death. He took her ashes to the Shack. Robert built the Shack as a crude hunting shack on Foster Lake, the only privately owned lake in the state. Always the prankster, he put a stuffed badger on the floor of the outhouse, so when I opened the door of the outhouse, the badger's barred teeth scared the shit out of me.

After they married, she spent her summers at the Shack, and they doubled the size of the Shack and added indoor plumbing. Because he and Mom were often naked at the Shack, when Robert found a road sign with the name Tittabawassee on it, he nailed it to a post at the entrance. I took a picture of it. The chipmunks at the Shack knew her so well that when her car pulled up, they gathered around the front tires waiting for her peanuts.

I, my brothers, and her sister went to the edge of Foster Lake, there was no dock. We bent down, and I looked around. No one was going to volunteer to scatter her ashes, so it fell to me. John had the box with her ashes. I put out my hand, and he gave me the plastic bag that opened easily. I reached in, took a handful, and sobbing I spread Mom across the face of Foster Lake.

My grandfather, John Forester, died young of a heart attack, and until the day he died, Dad obsessed over dying from a heart attack. He had an early cholesterol problem, but colored margarine was illegal in the Dairy State, so for a year he smuggled cases of colored margarine from Illinois to Wausau. He had weak fingernails, so for a year, I ate Jell-O every day because he thought it would harden his fingernails.

He skied until his seventies, and he golfed until his eighties. He did that with John, but he never did them with me. I'm OK with the golf part because I think it's a silly sport, and my memories of skiing are sitting constipated on an ice-cold throne in a ski lodge, but I still resent that he did not do them with me.

In 1979, when he was in his sixties, he had a pig valve replacement done at the Cleveland Clinic. He was told the valve would last twenty-five years; it lasted longer. When he was ninety-three, Dad said, "This is enough." He died in his sleep in 2008, age ninety-five, having spent the prior evening wearing one of his many brightly colored sports coats while having dinner with his favorite granddaughter.

I forgave Dad because he did what he was capable of. I was determined to have my own life, and he paid for it.

There was a service for him at the senior living community where he lived in Stuart, Florida, and a second service at the Universalist Church that I grew up in in Wausau. In our eulogies, John talked about Dad the athlete and the times they spent skiing. I talked about his initial discomfort with a gay son, but how he came around to accepting me. The reception afterwards was awkward because I knew none of them.

His ashes and Alice's, which were kept since her death in the Yawkey mausoleum in the Pine Grove cemetery, were taken to Point O' Pines by stepsister Leigh, the oldest child in Alice's family of four children; she's the bossy one.

Point O' Pines was Alice's summer residence starting in 1950. In the 1960s, she and Dad tore down Cyrus Yawkey's Victorian, and they replaced it with a California-style home that they kept enlarging. Standing in the volleyball court, Leigh gave me a bag of ashes containing both Dad and Alice ashes.

When I scattered Dad's ashes mixed with hers at Point O' Pines, Dad abandon his family for the last time. I resent I was asked to do that.

The remains of my parents rest on property owned by my stepparents' families, a telling sign of my destroyed family. The Forester family leaves no trace in Wausau aside from Dad's name on the donor wall of the Leigh Yawkey Woodson Art Museum. It's ironic that the obituary for Dad online does not mention Alice, and I found no obituary for him in the Wausau Daily Herald.

Yawkey Woodson family secrets were meant to stay secret.

I still have my genetic family. My Quarles family goes back to William Quarles in England in 1640 and my counterpart Charles Quarles Kamps lives with his wife in Milwaukee.

Get the Hell Out of Town

I had nothing in common with the kids in Wausau, and my homelife wasn't mine because of Dad's affair. In 1959, I heard of a Liberal Religious Youth (LRY), the youth organization of the Unitarian Universalist Church, weekend retreat for teens. The heavens opened and celestial light encircled me, Grant Wood-style. This was just what I'd been waiting for. The break to get the hell out of town.

My takeaway from the conference was that teens who were as smart as me with more interesting lives were Democrats. I desperately wanted friends, but according to the way I'd been raised by my Republicans parents, Democrats were a despicable lot. That didn't make sense. Someone was lying, and I started questioning what I was taught.

The LRY youth retreat, unlike Baptist Bible camp, was run by teenagers. The adult advisor signed the checks, and teens did the rest. The year I was president of the North Star Federation, I picked the venue, decided on the retreat program, chose the food service, and ran the conference with a guest list of anyone who wanted to be there. Jesus was absent, and the most heated debate in 1961 was whether Red China should be permitted to join the UN.

The LRY I knew was organized around regions across the United States and Canada, like the Western regions of Wisconsin, Minnesota, and the Dakotas that hosted my first conference. The four annual continental conferences I attended had teens from across North America boarding trains and busses excited to see old friends and jazzed to make new ones, maybe have a boyfriend or a girlfriend for a week.

For my second continental conference, four of us crammed into a 1953 VW Bug with all our luggage on top. We drove non-stop from St. Paul to outside Seattle. On Montana inclines, the VW air-cooled engine suffered mightily like the Little Engine That Could, but she made it. I was crushed in the Bug, but my excitement about getting to my second continental conference made the sixteen hundred miles feel like a joy ride. For another conference, I joined fifty Midwesterners in Chicago's LaSalle Street Station. Throughout the night from Chicago to Springfield, Massachusetts, we commandeered a New York Central coach. My only contact with the outside world was American Bandstand, and I envied the boys with ducktails, so as I crossed the country that night, I smoked cigarettes and stuck hipster poses.

My most poignant memories of the conferences are blending my voice with a hundred voices as we sang from songs the *Young Socialists Song Book* in a natural outdoor amphitheater. It was the first time I belonged to a tribe because they were more like me than the kids in Wausau. The other was watching the pink, yellow sunrise in a green Iowa cornfield on a hot muggy morning with two eighteen-year-olds from Davis, California. I had never seen anyone that comfortable in his skin. I didn't understand how they could just be themselves. I made them gods from a glamorous galaxy, and I wanted to be them so bad it hurt.

Three teens in LRY one a redhead turned me on. This was the fifties, so I didn't mess around with them afraid that if they knew I was homo they'd think less of me.

The UUA Church headquarters was situated on Beacon Street, cheek by jowl with the Commonwealth of Massachusetts's Capitol. When I walked the floors of the headquarters, I walked floors Ralph Waldo Emerson and his friend Ellery Channing, a noted theologian, walked, and the history of the church welled up in me.

At a Midwest leadership conclave on a sweltering summer evening, I spouted spontaneous poetry as I wandered the campus of University of Chicago. My inspiration was Lawrence Ferlinghetti's *Coney Island of the Mind*. I wish I'd kept the poems because I thought they were fucking amazing.

Fast forward to Climax, North Carolina, a real city. The LRY board meeting in Climax was my last board meeting as the President of the Board. The youth advisor, Peter Baldwin, initially wanted Vernon Grizzard to be president, but he declined. In 1968, Vernon, a draft resistor, went to North Vietnam to protest the war with Tom Hayden. I thought draft resisters had amazing courage, and Vernon became my James Dean rebel hero.

Unitarian Universalism believes in the goodness of everyone. I lived harrowing times, but it kept my faith in a better future intact.

What I learned about life in LRY is as much a part of me as my inherited genes.

29

The Sixties

Big D Mistake, 1962 - 1966

I was the smartest kid in high school, and teachers called on me because I was wanted to learn. I never had homework, although I did draft the most comprehensive papers in history classes. The only test I studied for was a final biology exam. Mom gave me a diet pill to help me stay awake, and I aced the test. High school was a breeze because my mind was never challenged, and in Wausau being intelligent wasn't seen as an asset.

That was not good enough for Dartmouth. I wasn't the smartest kid in my class, and I felt out of place. Getting that far from Wausau wasn't the East Coast excitement I thought it would be because Dartmouth was just as cold as Wausau.

I was certain an Ivy League college would be sophisticated, and my just being on the campus by osmosis I would learn the trick of being me and no one cared.

I was mistaken. Puritans founded Dartmouth, and the

college never thought it needed staff that could reached out to men like me who were confused about our sexuality. They were just as backwards around sexuality as the people of Wausau When John F. Kennedy was assassinated, I was in Dick's House, the campus hospital. If Norman Rockwell needed the perfect small-town hospital for his next *Saturday Evening Post* cover, Dick's House was that hospital. It was painfully neat and tidy. I doubt any of the doctors that treated me ever heard the word gay.

I majored in government because I thought government was the key to making social change, and because power fascinates me. For an exam, I memorized eleven statements that best captured that political movement. Few of the other classes got me that excited. I was a miserable failure in the creative writing class, and the only professor who took a personal interest in me was the young professor of my Indian Government class. He invited me to his home for dinner. He and his wife lived in Bombay and using spices from India, she introduced me to Indian food, and her ready supply of yogurt kept my mouth from burning up.

With Dartmouth miles from women, campus life was a sea of frustrated testosterone.

I have exacting standards for the people in my life, and they applied to homos even though I didn't know what a homo looked like. Bill lived down the hall. He asked me to give him a backrub. I came to Dartmouth with this cockamamy rationale for liking dick that college would be a watershed, because when Mom and Dad were in college, it was a watershed where they went from being kids to being adults. This was a time when being identified as homo would get you kicked out of our home and church, so I pretended college was going to rid me of my urges. I refused his offer of a backrub He asked a second time, and I refused him a second time. Then, the urges got the best of me, and I asked Bill. if he still wanted a backrub.

He turned on me as a beleaguered queen whose dignity had been compromised. I'd never seen that kind of behavior, and it scared the crap out of me. If that was gay, I wanted nothing to do with it.

Pouring salt on the wound, we were invited to dinner at the home of our advisor that very evening, which meant we'd be in close quarters at our advisor's home for an indetermined amount of time. He kept ten paces ahead of me as we trudged through knee-high snowdrifts. My advisor was a crusty, elderly Eastern European classics professor, and at our first meeting when I told him I was homesick, and he told me to study harder. He wasn't your warm, sensitive kinda guy and he was the last thing I needed. I expect Dartmouth would be wise to the ways of man and support its students as they grappled with becoming adults, and it failed.

With Bill next to me at the dinner table with lace doilies, I was on guard the whole time. I did my good student thing as I ate the pot roast and root vegetables I was served. My advisor in a dark wool suit and his wife in a faded red babushka were not chatty. There's nothing like a queen who feels trapped. Their indifference gave him a platform to spew all the "I don't know the creep sitting next to me" bullshit that popped up on the screen in his brain. While he was busy putting on his show of contempt, I faded into the drapes mesmerized by the babushka.

One of the leading actors on campus, and one of the few effeminate men on campus at an all-male school, told me if I wasn't in his room at eleven, he would commit suicide. I had the presence of mind to tell him to talk to a therapist. The third piece of the drive me into the closet trifecta was a man with no redeeming qualities from Dayton, Ohio, who tried to put the make on me.

I wanted a real man and none of them made the cut.

My four years at Dartmouth were wasted.

Grown Ups, 1966-1968

Philadelphia was my first big city and my first home was a row house. The city was a large industrial center, but it was an easy city to live in. The colonial part of the city had been restored with cobble stoned streets, so it looked much like it did in the 17th century. I walked the street Thomas Jefferson walked the day he delivered his Declaration of Independence to the waiting Continental Congress. Standing in the entry of Independence Hall, I felt its history because I was standing where men a few years older than me crafted the most important documents in America, the Declaration of Independence, and the Constitution. I was caught up in their revolutionary thinking and wondered did they have the same impulse to stop Britain's tyranny that I had to stop the war in Vietnam?

My coming to Jesus moment was Jane Jacobs' book *Death and Life of Great American Cities*. She celebrated the cultural wealth of cities that was diametrically opposed to me being protected from the outside world. She argued that old neighborhoods are more than rundown buildings; they are living, breathing organisms soaked with strands of culture.

The inner city is a web of beliefs, diverse ways of living, and traditions that can't be picked up and moved. When inner cities are destroyed by redevelopment, so are the cultures that lived there. The corner store run by a family for the last thirty years is more essential to the health of a community than a brand-new community center because people's history in a place affects how they interact with each other in that space.

Gay men in the 1960s didn't favor alleys because they liked the smell of garbage; they favored them because alleys were safe from the cops' prying eyes, a safe space where they could go down on each other in peace.

The redevelopment of urban core cities that started in the sixties with millions of federal dollars was heralded as the restoration of central cities, but their reality disrupted Black culture, destroying some of it completely like the Western Addition blocks from my home that was destroyed by the San Francisco Redevelopment Agency.

I brought a lifetime of upper-middle-class attitudes to my work, and they colored what I thought. I had to recognize them before I started thinking about state or federal programs that could make the lives of people in poverty more rewarding

My first lesson in that was Bill Grigsby asking the housing class. "What do poor people want?"

Hands shot up. "Better housing!" "Safe streets!" "Childcare!"

He deadpanned, "They want a Chevy and a house in the suburbs."

Before I even tried to be effective in someone else's life, I had to recognize that poor people are just like everyone else, and I must treat them accordingly.

The studio class was the first time I felt engaged in a class; I was so taken by it I couldn't wait for the next class. It started the first day with Paul Niebanck, balding and nearly blind, announcing, "I am splitting the class into teams, and Chuck will lead one." He went on to name other team leaders. I was taken aback because no one had respected my abilities since LRY.

Besides boosting my ego, his class revolutionized my idea of education because for the first time I was asked to think for myself and solve a problem without a textbook in real-time. It was exhilarating because I could take risks without being afraid of failing and I could learn from my mistakes. I could act with the freedom to act that I had when I was in LRY

Each team's assignment was designing a sustainable community for a stranded group, and my group was stranded on a tropical isle. My instincts were good when picking my team: John Crossman, an engineer; Dennis Ryan, an architectural designer; Martha Bailey, who was familiar with social work; and Jerry, another designer.

I thought my degree in government paled compared to their interests and education; I was in over my head because they knew the importance of open space to housing and the relationship of fresh food to mental health, but they respected my judgment and they looked to me to for decisions.

After months of designing a community on a tropical isle where I'd vacation if I could get there, my contribution was, "If they don't have to work at surviving, they'll get bored, and things will soon turn nasty." That was not me projecting, because if a stranded group does not have to concentrate on finding food and shelter, they will have nothing to do. Eventually, someone will claim a certain part of the beach as theirs. Arguments about whether anyone has the right to claim anything arise and then someone claims another part of the beach, and before you know it, they are going at each other tooth and nail.

If the people on my isle did not deal with boredom, years later a passing ship would find the isle's beaches awash with well-fed bodies and evidence of blunt force trauma.

I was awarded a stipend for the summer between terms to collaborate with the disadvantaged. That summer I helped Philadelphia set up its first Model Cites program in an old office in North Philadelphia surrounded by blocks of abandoned, derelict buildings. The neighborhood was once home to the city's Irish and Jewish immigrant middle classes. Walking around the neighborhood, I felt the pulse of Philadelphia's most distressed.

After work, in a local hangout over a beer, I absorbed what I've seen that day which was a lot because I had never seen poverty like the poverty of North Philadelphia. I had a tough time wrapping my head around families that survived in a derelict vacant building with no plumbing or electricity. What amazed me was their resilience. Hearing their churches ring out in song gave me hope they would someday be accepted as equals.

At the end of summer, I thought homeownership would improve the lives of the poor, but a professor accused me of being a Communist. Even if such a homeownership program were funded, it would be stymied by the insurance companies and banks that red-line neighborhoods and charge minorities higher rates for mortgages. Their insidious practices perpetuate poverty.

Paul taught me to think holistically, to think on my own, and to believe in myself. To understand why another person thinks the way they do. Where are they coming from? What makes them feel that way? Paul made a huge impression. He remained a friend and a generous correspondent until his recent death. His way of thinking continues to guide me, and I am forever grateful to him.

My destiny was a big city, and now I lived in a major metropolitan city rich in history and culture. Quakers founded Philadelphia, and I was honored to be living where the Quakers' openness gave birth to the nation when the Declaration of Independence and the Constitution were written and signed there. Philadelphia's street pattern of four squares laid out in a gird by William Penn became the model for street patterns in cities across the country.

As a major Atlantic port and rail gateway to the West in the 19th century, Philadelphia accepted thousands of Brits, Germans, Russians, Irish, Italians, and Poles as they moved to America for religious freedom, to avoid starvation, and for better-paying jobs. They enriched the culture.

As an industrial center in the first half of the 20th century, Philadelphia attracted share-crop Black farmers from the South seeking better-paying jobs and freedom from their oppressors. Their culture blended into other cultures giving the city the rich mosaic of neighborhoods that makes a big city an exciting place to live.

I fell in love with the brick row houses around Rittenhouse Square. The delicacy of the woodwork is a testament to the prosperity of the families that built them and the prosperity of the time they were built. I thought they were the finest residential arrangement because they maximized interior space in a limited area elegantly. My San Francisco Edwardian looks like a row house.

Coming from Wausau with its single minority, I fell in love with Philadelphia's urbanity. When Suburban Station flooded the city with Main Line middle-and upper-class white commuters on their way to the city's skyscrapers downtown, a mix-race rower glided across the Schuylkill River, no different from the rowers that Eakins painted in the 1870s. When a white woman dropped her mixed-race son off at a Quaker school in Germantown, a young mixed race Black man was taking his Black grandmother to a beauty parlor in Carroll Park. And while they are doing that, a third-generation Italian swept the soot off his South Philadelphia stoop. That ethnic richness was where I thrived.

Philadelphia's mix of fine museums spoke volumes about the pride the people of Philadelphia had for their city. Their generosity built the magnificent yellow-stone Philadelphia Museum of Art that sits proudly at the base of a magisterial boulevard. If I stayed there years, I wouldn't have had time to appreciate its magnificent collections. The Barnes Collection was one man's tribute to the post-impressionists. Benjamin Franklin started the Library Company in Philadelphia, the first library in America.

Wealthy donors bequeathed the Rodin Museum to the city. Standing at the foot of The Thinker, I was astonished that Rodin was able to create humanity from bronze. How did he see the figure, and when did he know he'd done enough? I wanted to cuddle him and lie at the feet of Balzac, and let his words wash over me.

Philadelphia gave me license to admit I'm an artist that I dismissed as a kid in Wausau because I did not want to be seen as effete. Great art with its pain on canvas, its fascination with flight on handmade rice paper, and a lover's passion in marble fill me with hope for a better future.

Philadelphia also changed the way I think about food. My culinary history started with a small plastic bag of fenugreek tied with string. I developed my taste for raw oysters. Reading Terminal Market was a culinary cathedral with parishioners worshipping at altars of fresh fruits and vegetables, the finest cuts of meat, and straight from Chesapeake Bay seafood. I could spend a mouthwatering day there and not sample everything but still go home with a bellyful of goodness. My favorite was Bassetts Lancaster County ice cream, a rich and creamy mix of buttery magic. There's always a line.

The 9th Street Italian Market blew me away. I'd never seen anything like it, never seen people so obsessed with food. The market was home to generations-old Italian restaurants, stalls with mountains of colorful spices, and clotheslines with embroidered blouses. It had its own churches, schools, and the freshest produce in the city. Standing in the middle of the street, I was part of a moving mass from multiple social classes that treated each other as family. The sense of the place excited me, and much as I wanted, I couldn't take the large Italian woman making porcini mushroom pasta home with me.

The big city let me have an affair with a classmate. His kiss in a lace curtain bedroom in New Canann, Connecticut told me I was gay. No more pretending and no more excuses. I am gay. A lifetime of walls came crashing down around me and I was blinded by the light of reality. There was no turning back.

We were power cuddlers and inseparable for months. Every time I suggested we move in together, he changed the subject. After two months of that, I'd had it with trying to be gay. I asked Christine Webb, who I'd traveled Europe with to move to Philadelphia. We married a year later. Our honeymoon two months before we married was a week in Montego Bay, Jamaica, with Dow Stewart, a chum from Dartmouth, and his wife.

My class mostly because of Paul Niebanck was one of those classes that other classes talk about. The class of sixty-eight is a legend Many of the class end up in Seattle. Paul had an undersecretary job in the federal government. He headed one of the experimental colleges at UC Santa Cruz, and his last home was in Seattle. John Crossman married Elsie, a Panamanian classmate, and they have a son and daughter and they lived in Seattle. He worked to retirement at a federal labor agency, and Elsie worked at the City Planning Department. Dennis Ryan married Trixie Farrar a classmate and a Team leader and they had two sons. They first lived in San Francisco, and if it weren't for them, I wouldn't have this life. They moved to Seattle where Trixie worked for the City Planning Department. She was good with the details and knows patience with commission meetings. Dennis had a position at the University and rose to eventually head the department. Trixie had an affair with the man who owned the Mercedes dealership. When she and one of her sons were driving to their second home on Whitbey Island the car went off the road. Trixie died, but the son lived. Several other of my Penn classmates live in Seattle.

Christine and I joined the Peace Corps in 1968, and we were sent to Santiago, Chile where I was promised work with city planners, but that never happened. I was relegated to office work at an innovative self-help housing community. In the evening I handed out surplus US rice and powdered milk to the people who lived in the community. I built a four-room house on my own. It had a propane stove and small refrigerator but no radio or TV. The social worker that Christine was supposed to work with never showed up, so she had a lot of free time. She didn't understand the difference between pounds and kilograms when ordering a chunk of beef. Beef was rationed in Chile; it was only sold half the month. The amount she bought would have fed a family of five for weeks because they would have used small bits in soup and news of being rich Americans quickly circulated. Because we spoke English around the house and with our ex pat friends, my Spanish was only good enough to argue with micro drivers, small van like busses.

With a lot of time on my hands during the day, I saw a lot of Hollywood movies six months after they were released in New York and Los Angeles.

Chilean men in the poblacions, the poorer neighborhoods weren't great beauties, and I befriended Mario, a European handsome man who looked like young Brando. He and his wife Maria, another beauty with gorgeous Long black hair right out of a Pedro Almodova movie, lived in our quadrant. He invited us to join them for a weekend at her parents' vacation home built on sand in the port city of San Antonio.

Our first night in the house, as I lay in bed with Chirstine, the clams we bought at the wharf opened, making a popping sound, and I imagined Mario gently slipping in beside me. I wanted him so bad that his touch as I lay there felt like an actual touch.

A beautiful young man I met in an art gallery invited me to lunch with his family in their luxurious apartment on Parque Forrestal. After a delicious meal and warm conversation with his generous family, he asked to see me again. I wasn't out, and the thought of ending up in a South American prison had me begging off. He was so sweet; I want to think that he's now living with a Chilean gentleman in Vina del Mar. They sit on the deck and watch the passing whales. I think about what I would have done if I'd been out when that happened

A less attractive man did something to my backside in a theater men's room. I would have known if I were penetrated. While he spewed rapid fire Spanish behind me he did something and came; I suspect he was jacking away as he spewed Spanishl

Chile is one of the few living democracies in South America. They also have a sense of humor. There were twelve newspapers when I was there, and each had its own political slant. They take politics seriously. Every election, cards are made with the image of each candidate. When your friend's candidate loses, you attach a tail to his candidate's image and give him the card. No one has an AR47 or a glock; the card says it all. Compare that the way the Trump dealt with his loss.

I was in Chile for a national election. A friend on a Ford Foundation fellowship was there studying the history of the Socialist Party in Chile. He knew people inside Salvadore Allende's campaign. Traditionally, the popularity of candidates for a president are measured by the size of their crowd at a march in Santiago that are held on separate days just before the election. The Allende campaign did the first polling in Chile, and they found Allende was ahead but not by much. They feared if the centrist candidate was seen as weak, his followers would go with the conservative candidate. To correct the imbalance, they packed the parade of the centrist candidate. When the demonstrations happened within days of each other, the crowds looked the same, and Allende won by a narrow margin.

Richard Nixon's State Department saw Allende as another Fidel Castro and they pulled the Peace Corps out of Chile.

Since I never got work as a city planner, I was happy to leave a few months short of my contract. We moved to San Francisco in January 1971, and Seth was born four months later.

A year after Allende was elected, conservative elements in Chile assisted by the CIA staged a coup, and when they occupied the Palacio de La Moneda, Chile's White House, Salvador Allende committed suicide. The coup quashed a democracy and a symbol of hope for the people of South America. An authoritarian military dictatorship led by Augusto Pinochet ruled Chile for seventeen years. I was there five years ago, and the difference was amazing. Santiago looked like a modern city with miles of skyscrapers and the nicest neighborhoods on the outside has kept moving out. Providencia was close to the edge when I was there. It's now closer to the center than it is to the edge. The Palacio de La Moneda Chile's White House was covered with soot when I lived there, but when I came back, I didn't recognize it because it had been restored to the original white.

San Francisco in the 1970s

My Coming Out Story

In 1971 I met Jack Garcia at a crummy gym near City Hall. While I was still married, we spent a weekend in the Gold Country, where I spent most of the time in a woodsy motel having my first gay sex. He tried to fuck me, but I was tight. We didn't just fuck. We went to Calaveras Big Trees state park where standing next to a giant sequoia I realize how insignificant I was in the great scheme of things. When we got back to the motel, we had more sex.

I moved into Jack's home in the Oakland Hills on a Thursday. Saturday morning, he said he was going to a party that night, and I wasn't invited. I was out for just four days, and he was going into the city to have an S&M experience. My abandonment issues went wild. I badgered him all day, and he finally confessed he was going to an S/M party, but I didn't know anything about S/M.

It got worse. Not only was he into something that scared the crap out of me I was being abandoned a bridge away from everything familiar. Being alone in a strange house scared me. We finally agreed, I'd go into the city with him, and he'd drop my off on Castro Street where Toad Hall had just opened. He would go to his party not far away. We would meet at midnight at the corner of Market and Castro, and he'd take me home.

I stood across from Toad Hall, now part of Walgreens, for half an hour, amazed at the audacity of men who went into Toad Hall. I thought you needed a password, but they got through the heavy oak door as easily as they get through the glass door at Cliff's Hardware.

I screwed up my courage and went inside. I was adjusting to the unfamiliar environment, when a man with Hollywood good looks in a red sweater asked me to go home with him. I was meeting Jack at midnight, but my pride wouldn't let me be outdone by Jack, so. I made a date with Red Sweater for Tuesday.

Tuesday was the beginning of my trial by fire. Red Sweater was a teacher, and he spent the first hour with me in his Castro apartment on the phone with a long cord with an irate parent. Meanwhile, I was fending off his roommate with thick lips. Once in the bedroom, he stripped to red bikini underwear and announced that he wanted me to fuck him. My dick barely knew him, and it had never fucked anyone, so it curled up and went to sleep.

The Universe provided with rare snow that happens once a century in San Francisco. The snow gave me an excuse to stand at the window and watch snowflakes make a halo around a streetlight, long enough to make a polite exit.

It got worse. For the two following Saturday nights, I went to the Ramrod, Jack's favorite leather bar. I was there the first time for fifteen minutes, and it was clear that Jack was going to take a man home from, and he didn't want me to be there. My crash course in cruising that started immediately was going home with a short German who wanted me to bite him. It didn't get better the next time. This time, Crash Course 101 meant going home with a larger white man, and he wanted me to choke him.

I freaked out. If this was gay life, I was screwed.

Jack said if I went to the bar on Sunday, he wouldn't go home with a man. I didn't want to go, but I didn't know gay etiquette, and I didn't want to offend the man who brought me out, so I went.

I got there, and *Gentlemen Prefer Blondes* with Jane Russell and Marilyn Monroe was being projected on a sheet in the back of the bar, and the brutes in leather that scared the crap out of me the first time, were sashaying like drag queens and singing along like drunk sorority girls. I was in shock because men in leather are supposed to be hardened men.

Jack stepped outside with a man in a leather jacket, and I bolted out the door and stormed down Folsom Street. It was a dark and an unfamiliar part of town, but the Universe provides. The first bar was the Stud.

It was almost empty and soft music was playing, light years different from the Ramrod. Maybe there was a good gay bar. I ordered a glass of wine.

A man with blond hair down to his butt in a green, tartan flannel shirt halfway down the bar got up and asked to buy me a glass of wine. He didn't look like the men in the Ramrod, and when he said his dog was waiting in the car, I knew he was my savoir. I said yes. He drove me and his dog to his bungalow in El Cerrito. In his living room with a low ceiling and the mounted head of a bear, he gave me a beer and mescaline.

We started making out on mound of pillows. and we'd been at it for some time when my hand grazed his crotch. Like a cartoon, time stopped with a big, white explosion. I'd never felt anything that big. I had to touch the sleeping giant inside his jeans several times before I could admit that my hand was on top of a juicy monster cock.

I'd never sucked a dick, so you can imagine how hard it was for me to put my mouth around his Goliath, but I'm a trooper. He was a gentleman and drove me back to Jack's house. I returned to the Stud the next Saturday hoping to repeat the magic. There is more about the Stud and what happened with Clay Grillo that I met at the Stud elsewhere in this memoir

In my first year out, my naïve stereotypes of a gay man were shattered every time I went home with a man like the man who was about to spend a year as wig master for Peter Jackson's *Lord of the Rings* movie production company in New Zealand.

Golden Gate Park was the site of two cruising areas, one around the windmill the Dutch government gave the city and another in the bushes closer to Ocean Beach. I never cruised there because park sex isn't my thing.

I could indulge my interest in another culture by spending an afternoon in North Beach along Columbus Avenue, gorging on a cannoli at the Victoria Bakery and reading Alan Ginsberg's *Howl* in City Lights Bookstore.

Chinatown with its narrow backstreets was a Chinese puzzle and I feared entering it. Peking ducks in their glistening splendor hung in windows like a continuous train of gold on Stockton Street, and Grant Avenue looked like a street in Beijing with shops selling gold bracelets and models of the Chinatown Arch.

Twenty-fourth Street in the Mission with its street vendors

of fresh from the farm produce and plump ripe fruits reminded me of the street vendors in Chile, and I ate a heaping plateful of fried beans and carne asada at a Mexican restaurant, with its windows on the street lined with colored Christmas tree lights.

I'd never seen a city where people were spontaneously generous. Alice had gazillions of Yawkey money, and Dad made sure they were there every time she looked at her bank account; none of my four parents were spontaneous. In northern Wisconsin if you were spontaneous, you'd do something stupid and could end up freezing to death. I didn't think I had it in me to be spontaneously generous.

I learned by watching others. An example was buying flowers for the Richard when he invited me to dinner. I'd never done it, but I did it because when Clay came to dinner, he brought me handful of flowers.

What stands out from the first Castro Street Fair are five twenty-year-old, gorgeous men naked from the waist. They formed a wedge of masculine beauty. I'd never seen that much pulchritude. It would make a great stamp.

In 1973, I'd been out a year, and I stopped in the middle of Civic Center Plaza beneath an olive tree. In the past week, I went to the bars at nine, I played with a man until one AM. I got up at seven AM. I repeated that routine not just every night that week, but for every night for the two prior weeks.

I had to decide: Did I want to do what Dad wanted me to do and eventually become the Director of Planning, or did I want to be sexually active? The choice was clear.

If I did everything necessary to became the Director of Planning, I would be active in civic organizations like San Francisco Beautiful and San Francisco Bay Area Planning and Urban Research Association. I'd be staying up to date with changes in the profession as I rose through the ranks of the American Planning Association. My time out of the office would be spent socializing with other planners and straight people in San Francisco who had a civic bent. They were good people. I'd play golf.

At fifty, when he said I could start enjoying life, I wouldn't be as attractive as I am now, and I'd have less energy and I'd regret missing thirty years of touching men that makes me feel complete.

That day in March, I made the conscious decision to be a sexually active gay man.

San Francisco in the seventies was the best time in history to be a gay man. The city exploded with joy, with waves of happiness washing down sidewalks. It was a democracy with no rules, and no underpinning of tradition because none of us had ever lived as an out gay man.

San Francisco was the perfect trifecta of cheap housing, a city tradition of nurturing outcastes, and plenty of open positions. My generation was the Glorious Migration because we were the first generation that lived without shame. The generations before us couldn't admit they were homos because if they did, they'd lose their job, their family, and their livelihood. They lived in constant fear. We said, "None of that! We're going to live our way."

My hero was the man living his dream, the man living how he wanted to live. In the carousel of sex without boundaries, my hero was the man who saw sex as a sport, and even though sex didn't have the pageantry of tennis, he honed his skills as he would for tennis.

It was a time when nothing was out of bounds and having sex was the norm. Beneath that, I did the important work of learning what it means to think and act like a gay man.

Free to be me didn't just happen. I didn't cross the city limits and suddenly, I could have as much sex as I wanted. I had to learn how to navigate a sexual world without barriers which is tricky, and I had to rethink dictums about sex that I took for granted. I had stop thinking I was a freak.

Coming out as sexually active was the hardest because I thought stripping away what I loved would set me back. When I admitted I need sex, the shit was gone. That's it; the shit was gone, and a tsunami of relief washed over me. Adjusting to my newfound sexual freedom posed a challenge because while sexual freedom surprised me by its suddenness, it involved rejection.

My decision to admit I need sex was an amazing breath of fresh air.

I started having sex on a regular basis. Having a man inside me was like nothing I'd ever done. Feeling him dick was a closeness that was reassuring, and I wanted more of him. I loved the tingling sensation and the sound of his dick as it went in and came out of me, a music of the street, the music of sensual reality. Other times we were a bundle of hot sex, rolling around each other. I couldn't believe anyone could make he feel that ecstatically happy. I was on fire. At some point I realized it wasn't just me, because when the men I went home with had sex, the took on a sex persona every time we played. It wasn't there at first, but once I saw it, I knew I could do anything with him because he was in play mode. He looked different, his face and eyes were different, and I saw it every time we played. Seeing it meant I could be as sensuous I wanted, I could be a pig or a peacock.

Housing was cheap in the Seventies, so every chance I got, I moved to larger and cooler apartments with a better place to have sex, ending up with the perfect apartment for a gay man, the corner apartment in a Queen Anne Victorian on Diamond Street. The bathroom fixture had the right connection for a douche hose. The bedroom had good light, so when we woke in the morning, I could see the glow on his face after a night of intimate sex unlike the sex he usually had. The owner of the building was a sexy, Italian American gay man ten years my senior.

One of the benefits of sleeping around was accumulating ideas for decorating my home. San Francisco was a maelstrom of creativity, and the sex was raw because men were having multiple sex for the first time. As a savored the state I was in after having sex I thought I'd seen the most imaginative décor in one home, only to feel the same way the next time I stayed overnight with a man. The sex was hot, and their imaginations were out of this world.

Gay men my age and younger created magical kingdoms with little cash and fertile imagination. A man in North Beach covered an entire wall with Kraft paper that made it look like kidskin. In another apartment caged lizards and weird plants that looked like domes of bark with a single stem had pride of place in his living room.

I witnessed Castro Street as it went from just another San Francisco neighborhood commercial street with two donut shops, a title insurance company, Cliff's Hardware, Star Pharmacy. a second-hand furniture store, Toad Hall, and the Midnight Sun to a vibrant three-block area with the first gay-owned businesses, Tommy's Flowers, American Boy, The Patio Café, and Pascua café, now Starbucks. There were six gay bars and gay-owned Atlas Savings and Loan. The parishioners at Most Holy Redeemer went from being married Catholic couples and their children who were baptized in the church to gay lovers who fucked their brains out and lived together for the first time.

I couldn't believe the clerk at Cliff's was gay because clerks at hardware stores were straight. As the weeks went by, men like him were all over the place, but every time, I was surprised he was gay because he was supposed to be straight. Everywhere I looked, even unlikely places, I found another gay man.

Free from the strictures of the past, the Glorious Migration was the artists and teachers, bus drivers, and academics we wanted to be, no longer fearing being queer would kill our chances.

In 1971 a thousand gay men moved to San Francisco every month, so by the time I got to the party in 1972, every street throbbed with another freshly scrubbed face. I spent many glorious hours in the bars learning how to be gay, but when a man talked about real estate, it pissed me off because I was enjoying my Peter Pan existence, and I didn't like competing with his excitement at getting a fucking city permit. It took me years to realize most men don't have sex on their brain twenty-four seven.

The early Seventies was a cauldron of new ways of living and new ways of thinking about sex. It transformed the way gay men thought about sex. Sex isn't talked about for a host of societal reasons, but it left some of the Glorious Transformation without sound knowledge of sex or the emotional tools to deal with it when they arrived. I was impressed at how well we took care of them. Being the first generation to be out created the bond of us being in this together. Breaking rules and having sex made us a family of rebels for justice. A cottage industry of gay therapists built around a generation of men that were coming out simultaneously while meanwhile men were seeing sex as a pleasure they deserved. Sex was no longer that intimate act that you were afraid to confess they liked. Men owned their sex.

The Glorious Transformation, 1970-1974

The Glorious Transformation in San Francisco changed the way gay men saw themself lasted four years. Before 1970, gay men lived in fear. After 1974, gay men knew there was a city where he could live openly. It was a transformation because it changed the way gay men saw themselves and how they thought about sex. Before Clay Grillo I feared exposing my interest in men. When Clay touched me, I knew it was OK to be gay. Human touch told me if he is gay, then I can be gay. I didn't know where I was touching him, but it was exactly where I was supposed to be touching him, and when I touched him, his body slid into mine. We broke the barrier in my head. I was no longer afraid of saying I am a gay man.

The Castro we know today started with Toad Hall, now part of Walgreens. It was so popular, the line on Sunday of men excited to be with men like them for the first time in their life stretched around the corner and up 18th Street. Think of that for a moment. An entire generation that had not been able to be gay all their life gets its first chance to be gay. That's like an atomic bomb that's just been released into the atmosphere. They were starved for companionship. The shift was monumental because men had been waiting for that moment ever since they knew they were gay, and they were living their dream. We were slaves to old world thinking who'd been freed from bondage.

In a city of strangers, at first the bars scared me because I'd never seen men who were that comfortable with being gay. Once I knew how to cruise, the bars were the heartbeat of the community They were the sun the neighborhood orbited around. The bars were the be all and end all of gay life in the early Seventies. The bars were Grand Central Station, a hectic meeting place, and the best place for queer information. They were the only public place where we could be with each other and be gay. My generation got to know each other, and we taught each other what it means to be gay in the bars. No one bothered us in the bars. We wrote our culture on bathroom walls.

Toad Hall's rival up Castro Street the Midnight Sun, now a rainbow gift store, vied for the hearts of gay men. The creativity they fostered exploded throughout the community. Every man's home was an homage to his being free for the first time in his life. Their homes were often the least attractive part of the building because they were cheap, but with little cash and energized imaginations they made they magical. One year their exterior holiday ornamentations with a sleigh full of elves at Toad Hall and a line of nutcrackers at the Midnight Sun put Macy's Christmas windows to shame. An interior wall of Toad Hall was covered floor to ceiling with potted poinsettias.

The owners of Twin Peaks at the corner of Market and Castro Streets, two women, had the balls to cover an exterior wall of their bar with clear window glass, the first gay bar in the country to expose its clientele to passersby.

Moby Dick on 18th Street with a giant fish tank was the bar for when I wanted to be in the Castro, but I didn't want to be seen in the Castro. The Nothing Special lived up to its name, so I never got inside. Daddy's leather bar came and went because it wasn't as authentic as the leather bars on Folsom Street. The Pendulum around the corner on 18th Street catered to Black men and the white men who were attracted to Black men.

Toad Hall was my first gay bar. Michael opened the bar, and the Breakfast Club convened at eleven every weekday morning. The matriarch of the club, Cupcake, called everyone Helen. His well-to-do parents were aghast when they saw him in a Fifties UCLA gay protest, so for as long as he never graced the threshold of their Beverly Hills home. they paid him enough to get by. With his alcohol ruined face, his scraggly beard, and his drab caftans, he was the ugliest man I'd ever seen. The rest of the breakfast club were alcoholics around his age.

He died of alcohol poisoning, and Michael buried his ashes beneath a dogwood at his cabin.

Thursday night at the Jackhammer was red hankie night, and one night, it felt like old home week because it was Folsom Weekend. Fisters from Europe and North America were there, and I'd played with a bunch of them. I was always impressed with the number of sorted fisters who lived in Canada and northern Europe, more than I imaged; they kept coming. It was reassuring to know that I was part of a worldwide family. That night, I was the proverbial kid in a candy store picking the treat I went home with.

After dark, the six blocks of deserted and vacant light industrial buildings South of Market were a leather playground. The Ramrod, the No Name, Fe-Be's with a plaster statue of David in a motorcycle cap, and the Stud were the stars. Because it was night, it was hard to see, so the first time I was on Folsom Street, I identified a leather bar by the apron of big hog motorcycles parked in front of it. Folsom Weekend began as a small local event on one block of Folsom Street, and today it's the world's largest leather event that takes up four blocks of Folsom Street and some side streets.

The Stud, my favorite, was the world's crossroads of sorted men, artists, and thinkers, and sex was just as important to them as was being themselves. They were the crème de la crème of gay masculinity. The Castro clone wore motorcycle boots, jeans, and a hooded sweatshirt under a Levi jacket, and I thought drag shows were displays of internalized homophobia. homophobia. None of that worked for me, so I made my version of a sexually active gay man using Bill as my model. When a man's touch was authentic in a way that fit my image of a sexually active gay man, I incorporated that into my persona. Layer by layer, I became the man I am today.

With a Mediterranean climate I wore a leather jacket when I went to the bars. I lived the heyday of gay bars in San Francisco. There were twenty-two gay bars in San Francisco in 1973. They specialized, so I had a lot to choose from depending on my mood. Bars were my source of men to have sex with. Most men had homes, so we didn't need bar sex Bars were socializing the place we got to know each other. Every man's home was an homage to his response to a city that let him be free to be himself. Men with different tastes and ethnicities found comfortable bars that fit their tastes, and every pride brought us together as a rainbow community.

The Glorious Transformation transformed the way gay men had sex. Until then, sex was furtive, and it came loaded with shame. The Seventies changed gay men's relationship with their body; their body was now a friend, no longer the enemy. Sex was fun with no emotional strings attached. In a time of exploding joy, I was free to have sex for the first time in my life and not worry about being discovered. Men who were unaccustomed to having sex were surprised when I said I wanted to have sex with him, but no one objected. Before 1970, I could be arrested for hugging a man in public. Now it's a standard form of greeting.

The first man I went home from the Stud took me to his Twin Peaks home on stilts in a restored 1950 Plymouth coupe. I had my first gay sex with him in his bedroom that was painted aubergine. I'd never been in a restored car, and I'd never been inside a house on stilts and aubergine was a color I had never seen, so I thought I'd fallen down Alice's well. How could a man be that creative with that many elements of his life?

Clay Grillo

I met Clay at the Stud on a warm September night, and I could not believe that the most handsome man in the bar wanted to make a date with me. He was an authentic gay man I knew. Making a date meant he wanted to have sex with me. He was half English and half Italian. Tall and slender with smooth Italian skin with the rugged facial features of a Saxon warrior. His body was in constant motion, and he paid no attention to his long chestnut hair. He didn't need to because it was naturally perfect. He was a native San Franciscan, and I couldn't have asked for a better guide; he was a five-star guide. I found parts of San Francisco like the alleys in Chinatown that I would have never found on my own. Our first picnic was in the Presidio cemetery where I looked over the bay and passing ships eating a sandwich he made for me. Thanks to him, I ate my first pirogue in a Russian bakery in the Richmond.

Adjusting to the freedom to have sex was both smooth and complicated. Before Clay, touching my dick was a source of reassurance, but I couldn't talk about if for fear of being thought I was a pervert.

It was smooth with Clay. He was half English, half Italian. He'd been gay for years, and that made being gay easier for me. The night he christened me in the art of fucking happened in his bedroom that was at the back of the building with a sloped ceiling. I had to step down to get into his bedroom because originally it was a greenhouse. There were three high on the wall rectangles of glass, and Clay filled the boxes at the base of them with coleus making the room feel like a jungle. His waterbed occupied most of the room with space on one side big enough to stand, and space for a chair in front of it. He covered the waterbed with a yellow, red, and orange Indian bedspread making the room look like a pasha's palace.

I sat on the edge of the waterbed, my clothes in a pile near the door. He sat in front of me on a wooden chair.

His quietly observing me unsettled me. He took in as much of me as he needed. I was eager to learn from him who'd been gay since he was twelve.

He slowly got up and in slow motion came closer. Without warning me, he pushed me back on the waterbed and fell on top of me. The water in the waterbed was pushed to the limits so every time I sank into it, it sent waves back rocking me into him. He got behind me and massaged my hip, and after he'd warmed up my hip, he worked his way down my leg. I thought he was doing something to my ankle, but he was positioning himself. I was on my side with me thinking he's doing something else; but he slid his long, slender dick into me. I exploded in hurt. He calmly assured me it would feel better the next time.

During all the years I'd repressed sex, I thought about what having sex with a gay man would feel like. He gave me the chance to claim it, and I was an open field.

He was right, there was no pain the second time, and I liked having him in me. I liked it so much I wasn't satisfied until he'd fucked me a third time.

Sex is complicated because it comes with a web of highly charged emotions and a lifetime of being told that sex with a man is bad. What triggers those emotions is the great Mystery of Life. The smartest way for me to deal with that web was for me to be me. Authenticity at first was tricky because I was used to second guessing every decision like a crazy person. Once I accepted that I am a sexual creature and that I want to be touched, I was authentic, and that attracted authentic men.

Clay must have thought I was ready because he said I had to meet Bill Day and Jim Hickey. The first time I saw them at the Savoy Tivoli, there were so at ease and handsome, I thought they were straight. They were gardeners and living in San Mateo County. Once a week they attended a meeting for men who were coming out led by Don Clark, author of the first gay-positive book *Loving Someone Gay*.

Bill asked me if they could stay over at my place on Wednesday, the day of the meeting instead of driving to San Mateo. That meant they planned to have sex. In those days it as common to have sex first and then become friends.

The door to my apartment opened from the entry hall. On the left was a nicely sized bathroom with a ten-foot ceiling, a clawfoot tub with a douche hose, and pedestal sink.

The living room, bedroom, and kitchen made a circle, so I could take food from the kitchen to the living room either via the entry hall or the bedroom. The living room had a chair, a daybed I used as a couch, and a potted palm. The bedroom had enough space for a queen-size bed and a built-in cabinet.

The first night they stayed overnight, we sat on the floor. Bill was tall and Scandinavian blond; his eyes blue, He moved with confidence. Jim was shorter and dark haired with an air of mystery. He checked with Bill before removing his shirt. Bill kissed him and his look told me I should start taking off my clothes.

We were naked with my skin on fire when they gave me a two-man massage to relaxed me; they knew what they were doing. They worked all over me as a team with no jealousy and no part of me was out of bounds. Bill fucked me first with Jim behind me, making sure I was comfortable. Jim had to fuck me, and Bill put my head in my head in his lap, so while Jim held my legs in the air as he fucked me, Bill played with my nipples that I discovered that night are connected to my hole. They worked like a fine clock, every part of them was in synch with every other part of them. The precision of the way they touched me took me out of the world of worry. Then they fucked each other. Watching them was watching a work of art. They were tender and tough. They opened a new world of couple sex to me, new ways of communicating with a man, a new way of seeing a man and his lover interact when they've having sex.

They were so emotionally clean they reminded me of innocent kids playing.

I played with them separately. Playing with Bill, whose mother grew up close to where my mother grew up in Milwaukee felt like playing with my coach. Every move was teaching me how to have sex with a man. He coached me to be as proficient as he was. Jim was a fireball. He knew what he wanted, and he knew what he was going to do to me, and I just let him have me. There's power in numbers, and if they are OK with sex, I can be OK with sex. He taught me not to be afraid of sex. They became my model for a gay couple.

Zohn Artman was Bill Graham's go-to guy at Bill Graham Presents, the premier rock concert promoter. He called himself a wizard, another kid from the Midwest and a dear friend who opened me to the world of not taking life seriously; enjoy it. He thought it was funny I worked in politics when my life could be something that was good for my soul. He teased me to live up to my hippie aspirations, and he knew that world wasn't all flowers and love songs; there was hurt and rejection. His home was on property owned by Tom Waddell. The US Olympic Committee took Tom to court in 1982 because he called the first national display of queer sportsmanship the Gay Olympics. They won, and Tom changed the name to Gay Games.

His cozy home looked a Hobbit designed it, no right angles, soft surfaces, intense colors, wood everywhere, and high-quality weed. He epitomized laid back, yet when Bill Graham said, "We need this impossible thing to happen at the most impossible moment." Zohn said, "No problem, Bill. I've got it covered." He was my guide through the Age of Aquarius, removing me. from the chaos of local politics. He had a lifetime of stories about books that inspired him like Kahil Gibran's *The Prophet*. To me, his world seemed perfect, yet he ran ten times faster than most people, and he always had time for another crazy character.

To get me into his world, Zohn made sure I had the best seats for four concerts, Bette Midler, two Elton John and Pink Floyd.

When Bette and her Harlettes in bizarre headpieces and naughty costumes came on stage, I fell out of my chair because I'd never seen anything that outrageous, every sequin was perfect. I couldn't believe the energy that she poured into every set, and she kept doing it for ninety minutes. Elton sang "Candle in the Wind,' and I said, "That's my favorite song." Then we sang "Daniel," and I said, "No, that's my favorite song." He kept doing that through two concerts, each time singing all my favorite songs, and at every concert he was dressed completely differently in something unexpected wearing another pair of outrageous glasses. I was so close to the stage he seemed to be singing to me. Pink Floyd was a psychedelic experience. I was on acid, and that let me immerse myself in the smoke, the sound and being transported to their other worldly universe. To a time and place where no one pays bills. To a world where nothing matters. Every time I hear *Dark Side of the Moon*, I'm back at that concert stoned out of my mind because they let me live in the moment where I was free of hurts. I wanted to shout to the gods, "You have me!"

In those days, bartenders were our rock stars, and Michael was nominated for the Golden Didleaux Award as Bartender of the Year. They always had an answer when a tourist needed directions to Golden Gate Park or where could he buy a douche hose. I developed a routine. I could never predict if a bar was going to be fun. It depended on the mood of the bartender, the music and things that can't be explained. I knew by ten-thirty. I lived for the flawless nights because they made up for unseen smile and the rejections.

I went to the bars at nine. With three beers I was ready to approach a man. I was impatient, so I often initiated the conversation.

I made mistakes. I did wake and wonder the next morning, what did I see in him? When I saw him on the street later, however, I acknowledged him because we were all part of the game.

I started my night of cruising at Toad Hall. It was tame for me sexually, but it was also a cultural icon. That meant Toad Hall was the first bar that men from out of town sampled, so there was always the chance I'd see a new face. If I didn't find someone I wanted to have sex with at Toad Hall, I went South of Market, sometimes stopping halfway at The Rainbow Cattle Company. It was a laidback hippie-cowboy, boots, and flannel shirt bar. Men who'd moved to Sonoma County used it when they were in the city. They wanted sex, they were just more restrained than the locals.

The Stud was a crossroads of assorted men from around the world. It was my home for four years. I was invited to the bar's private holiday party, and when I entered in the back door, I was given tab of acid. Half the bar was carpeted with Oriental carpets, upholstered armchairs, and couches that looked like a Christmas living room. The walls in the other half were covered with blue paper that looked like ice, and mylar icicles suspended from the ceiling made the room look like a Christmas wonderland.

A gorgeous man I saw in the bars but was afraid to talk to was there. Men that beautiful, protect themselves with invisible shields. I never thought I could break through his shield, so I stopped wasting my time. I was surprised when he said he wanted to come home with me.

You can't tell a man by his appearance, and when he asked that casually I should have known there was a hitch. Turns out, he was a sloppy bottom. I try to be an equal opportunity player, but sloppy bottoms disgust me because they don't honor sex. He was not as a power bottom. Big difference. A power bottom treats his ass like a Hells Angel treats his Harley hog. He keeps it in working order and he likes showing it off. A sloppy bottom doesn't respect his body, and he depends on drugs.

The first time I encountered the trio of big men in opera stockings, glittered beards, and platform boots at the Stud in 1975, they crossed too many lines for novice me. Once I had some distance, I liked the idea of genderfuck because they were walking billboards declaring "I don't give a flying fuck what you think." They were also groundbreakers who dared go where gay men feared to go.

The Ambush was a dope smoking, laidback bar. Michael and I stopped there the nights we came back from a weekend at his cabin. One night, the man next me on a bench got fisted and no one noticed.

I got a lesson in appearance versus substance on a road trip to Laguna Beach my second year out. There were four of us. A. was the ringleader who went there all the time, and he was the chief cheerleader for Laguna Beach, a true believer. B. was smaller and not as attractive, and he took his cues from A. The third, John was and the only one I knew before the trip because we worked out at the same gym. He was the epitome of male beauty. His proportions were perfect, and his Northern European skin was flawless. He wasn't a big man, but his smooth muscles in just the right places more than made up for it. This was before Nautilus equipment, protein shakes and routines that have become assembly lines for six pack abs. I don't remember how I got roped into the road trip, but I was always up for a road trip, especially one with John

We drove down Friday night and checked into our motel around midnight. The next morning, I was raring to go. A knew the perfect place for a light breakfast that he timed precisely, so we had enough time to eat and get to the beach when the men were at their peak. For him beach time was a science. The beach was half a mile of men showing off the hours they spent in the gym.

The minute John took off his tank top, he was the center of attention. The muscle builders showing off were his fan club. When John stripped down to a Speedo, the game was over. I didn't stand a chance. I was insignificant and ugly. No one looked at me. I was stage scenery that no one would miss if I weren't there.

My dinner was a Cobb salad at classy café on the water. By the time we got in the car to drive an hour to LA to go to another of A's must-sees, an LA disco, I was wishing I'd never come. I wasn't a huge fan of discos, and I didn't need heavy traffic. Under the flashing lights of the disco, and a thousand cliché' addicted men crowded a warehouse, I didn't matter and even if I took off my top, I didn't fit in. The reason I never went to discos was because they were a lousy place to pick up me, and this disco was a forceful reminder.

I don't know if their intension was to get laid, but no one hooked up, so we drove back to Laguna Beach. A. wanted to make a last-ditch effort at the Little Shrimp bar. I didn't say anything, but why did he think his life was something I would emulate?

I got lost in the older crowd in the small bar, and when I was on the deck gazing at the sea, a man sidled up to me and said, "I'm lonely, would you come back to my motel with me?" I was thirty, he was in his early forties in decent shape. His reddish-brown hair was cut short, and the same color beard and mustache were professionally trimmed. His face was square, his eyes brown with just enough hair on his broad freckled chest.

He was a cinematographer about to shoot the movie *Shampoo* with Warren Beatty and Goldie Hawn. I don't get hyped around movies, so that didn't impress me. What did impress me was his interest in having sex with an equal. He was generous sexually, ferocious as a bottom, and he knew how to make my ass sing, he was a four-season fucker. Another treat were his pharmaceutical poppers; the bullets wrapped in string. The high I got from them was pure and strong. They kept us going 'til dawn.

Pharmaceutical poppers are illegal in the States, but I'm not the only gay man who's made the pilgrimage to Tijuana, Mexico, going from farmacia to farmacia buying a couple of months' supply of pharmaceutical poppers.

On the ride back to San Francisco, John had an excuse for not going home with someone and the others said nothing, amazed that I had had a spectacular night with a cinematographer. What started with me feeling ugly and not as attractive as John ended up with me the winner in the getting laid competition.

As a touch-hungry man, I was made for the baths because the baths were pleasure palaces. Everyone was there to have sex, and no one stopped me from having sex, the freest place to indulge my imagination. In an erotic world designed for pleasuring gay men, I experimented with new moves, and the moves I learned from the men I played with.

My history with the baths started when I was married, and I went to a men's spa in North Beach that had been discovered by gay men. I didn't do anything because the atmosphere was alien to what I knew. Naked men that excited me as photos made me uncomfortable in the flesh because nothing had prepared me for such a blatant statement of sexual freedom. I had a lot to learn and a lot of stereotypes to overcome. The Finnish Baths on Upper Market with cubicles was the first time I had sex in a bathhouse. I was scared at first, but the older man let me relax, and after we came, I was proud of what I'd done. The Ritch Street Baths was the first baths owned and operated by a gay man. It had one floor of cubicles big enough for a narrow bed. The bottom floor had lockers, a carpeted stepped video lounge, and a giant fish tank of colorful fish next to a yogurt café. It was my first gay bath house. I never went back because sex for me is personal. I want as much time as I can with the men I'm having sex with, but the players there were in it for numbers.

The Eighth and Howard baths looked like Ritch Street, only brighter colors. It was popular with young men who were looking for a good time. I stopped going there when the man in front of me at the ticket line was refused entry. The baths were freedom and denying someone is antithetical to freedom. Later, I was disappointed when I discovered that white gay men can be just as prejudiced against Black men as straight me.

The South of the Slot was called the Crystal Palace because of the rampant drug use, but it was the most certain place I would find a fister on Sunday. A tall handsome man who played tennis gave me MDMA, ecstasy, and I had one of the wildest fist sessions. He put me in positions I never imagined, and he went wild when I had my hand in him.

I used Animals that was popular with men into kinkier sex a couple times but the times I played there were mechanical. I was just going through the motions because the men didn't excite me. There was a bath house in the mission where I got an outstanding best blow job from a man who removed his dentures. His gums felt I was fucking a hot water bottle.

The baths captured the essence of the early 1970s in San Francisco. They epitomize sex and pleasure, the unifying elements of the era.

Michael A. Schoch

Michael

Michael was a carnival ride in a swan boat. The thrills came from forded a stream on our way to his cabin. They were sleeping under the stars. They were when he lay next to me. Raised in blue-collar California, Michael was destined for grandeur. He was ten when his life was destroyed. His mother, the bright shining light of his life, died of breast cancer, and he blamed himself for twenty years. We couldn't have been more different. He was blue collar who never went to college, but his dreams were grand; I was wealthy with two Ivy degrees, but I was downwardly mobile. He was he daytime bartender at Toad Hall, I worked for mayor Joe Alioto. Yet, we wanted the same thing. He wanted a man to love, and I wanted a man to spend the rest of my life with. He'd been gay his entire life, I wanted to know how to be gay.

At eighteen, Michael's Archie Bunker father, Harry, told

George who was sharing Michael's bedroom to get his sorry ass out of the house in ten minutes. Eight minutes later, with four hundred dollars between them, Michael and George bought a beat-up Chevy, and they drove through the night to San Francisco. When he was setback with Hep C, George was nowhere to be seen, and he survived on peanut butter and the Brussell sprouts he grew in the yard.

I was on my lunch break from City Hall. I seldom went into a gay bar during the day, but the Universe had plans for me. He was across the bar at Toad Hall, and I had to have him.

I tried twice to meet him at the bar, but each time I was just another customer. He and Lou Kief were selling the clock cases they made at a Castro Street Fair. When I introduced myself, I got a blank stare because he was on speed in another planet.

Gregg Coates was a member of the Sharon Street family where I hung out after work. He was dating Lou Kief, and he asked me if I would give him a ride to the cabin that Lou and Michael were building near Annapolis. California in far Sonoma County. I had Seth that weekend, so the three of us headed north on 101. We were on a two-lane road behind Warm Springs dam where the only sign of civilization for twenty miles was a solitary mailbox, Gregg said, "Michael won't be coming until Sunday, and he may be bringing his boyfriend. I turned the van around and was about to head back to the city when the Universe told me to chance it.

Two weeks before that, Michael and Lou were in the camper they slept in while the built the cabin. They split a Quaalude and Lou asked Michael his three wishes. Michael said, "I want a man, a son, and a helicopter so we can get to the cabin faster. When he stepped foot on the deck of the cabin that fateful Sunday, I was there, and Seth was playing with his plastic helicopter. Every time we tried to kiss on the back of the cabin where I'd been adding siding, Seth wanted me to play with him. We finally got the chance later that day. My teenage dreams of the man who would love me forever were hazy because I was unable to decide if he was a man who looked like my movie star hero Alan Ladd or if he was one of boys in high school that I lusted after. The minute Michael took me in his arms and kissed me, he was the man that I dreamed of as teenager, and I wanted to spend the rest of my life with him.

I didn't know what love was because there wasn't any in Wausau.

San Francisco gave me license to make my own life, and Michael was part of it every second. My love of him swamped me because I'd never known anything like it, and I let it consume me. I didn't try to understand what was happening; I let it happen. Life was more than making something or achieving something. Life was being with him. I had to learn how to be happy. One day I realized I'd been happy all week. I hadn't done anything to make me happy, I just was happy. The English muffin with pepper jelly tasted different and the air was fresher. It was a world where every day was an adventure, and no matter what I did or where I went, Michael was there beside me. My job was now the means that paid for my life with Michael.

I kept pinching my wrist to make sure that I wasn't living a dream. I eventually stopped thinking about how I could be so happy because it was getting in the way of being happy. I was certain we knew each other in a prior life.

We built our life as partners in a three-bedroom flat in Alamo Square. At the beginning, he got the commercial range he wanted. It took five men to get it up to our third-floor flat. His mother was over his shoulder when he cooked at that stove, and he showed me how to use the stove's salamander. The flat had one bathroom and a separate WC. I got the shower room I wanted. The original bathroom had a cracked line floor, a cheesy vanity, and an old tub. My shower room had hex tile walls and floor. It had two modern controls and modern shower heads with a permanent douche hose between them. It also had a classic vintage porcelain sink that I salvaged from another of my properties.

The tile guy told Michael he should have used colorful Mexican tiles in the shower room because the hex tiles made it look like a gym. I wanted it to look like a gym. When he asked what the permanent douche hose, Michael told him we used it to wash the dog we didn't have.

I had no experience entertaining. The entire time I lived in Wausau, the only guest in our home was a man from Finland who came to dinner once. He was in Wausau to observe the paper making process at the paper mills in Wausau. Alice kept her home in Wausau and Point O Pines for herself and her extended family. Her cook and the young women who looked after her four kids were the only outsiders. Michael loved treating guests to moments they remembered.

I kept being continually reminded that I had never known a man who fit me as perfectly as Michael. Every day, I found yet another way that we were meant for each other. We were both Pisces. We were both early explorers of our sexuality; at twelve he stood in front of his house and got picked up by men in passing cars and they had sex in the car; At thirteen, I got boys to strip down to their white cotton JCPenney underwear. He wanted to share his cabin with a man. I was more than happy to oblige. His passion was food, his plating superb, and I thanked him every day for his gift of food. I told him "I love you" every day.

Coming from an emotional desert, his concern continued to overwhelm me, and I had to stop and think. Do I deserve the love and attention that continuously pours from him? I never had to prove anything, he accepted me as the man I was. He was the most precious piece of my life, the most vital part. I did not want anything to ever change because I knew I couldn't exist without him: He was my life, my other half.

Michael dreamt big. A window in his apartment on Shrader Street when we first met was made entirely of crystal stemware.

Our first year together, Michal planned a surprise birthday party for me. Over the bar at Toad Hall, he and Robert Simon, the assistant manager of the Mark Hopkins Hotel hatched a plot. In 1976 Robert couldn't tell his boss that he wanted to rent the suite the King of Norway used the last time he was in town to gay friends, so they concocted a scheme that had us as two estranged ranching brothers from Chico who were reuniting for the first time in twenty years.

On February 23, 1976, Michael said he was taking me out to dinner, and I should wear my cowboy boots and Stetson hat. That made no sense because the only place where men wore cowboy gear was a bar with country western dancing, but it didn't serve food. I didn't know what was going on when he pulled his truck into the entry of the Mark Hopkings. We were greeted by a silver-haired man in a tuxedo with a plastic clip on his lapel identifying him as the assistant manager. He said, "We've been expecting you, Michael. Please follow me." He took me to an elevator marked private. When I get to the top, at one end of a long narrow corridor three secret service men in black suits guard the door. Vice President and presidential candidate Walter Mondale and his staff were behind the door.

As soon as I am in the suite at the other end of the hall

the only other door on that floor, Michael had me sit next to a Cellophane wrapped basket of fruit and a stack of telegrams. "Aren't you going to open them?" I was still in shock when I read the telegram birthday greetings from Toad Hall regulars. I had to explore the suite, so I wandered through both bedrooms and the two bathrooms as well as the patio off the living room checking out the décor and the furnishings. The view of the city from the top of the Mark Hopkins was spectacular. Wanting to make it a special night, he brought a fistful of drugs, but he forgot rolling papers. This was his first experience in a luxury hotel, and I got a kick out of watching him when I said, "All you have to do is call room service." Fifteen minutes later, a suave young man in gray livery and a round cap presented him with a silver platter with two packs of rolling papers. I was just getting comfortable with his surprise when uniformed staff wheeled in a cart with silver domes, and he proceeded to serve us dinner. The chateaubriand was served with Bearnaise sauce he made at the table, the wine a fine Pinot Noir. We were being watched because when Robert came to check in with Michael, he said the staff noticed a chair was moved. The table was set for the two brothers to sit on opposite sides of the table. I moved a chair, so we'd be sitting next to each other. We got stoned and started making out ripping off clothing. We'd had sex several times when I climbed the fire escape on the patio. I loved the irony of being at the top of the fire escape ladder in my underwear and spying on the smartly dressed straight married couples who were dining in the Top of the Mark restaurant because I had the upper hand.

The next morning, after we'd fucked each other silly in every room in the suite, I ate my favorite eggs over medium, four sausages, and hashbrowns as I read the New York Times in the solarium. I put on the suit Michael put in the closet of the main bedroom and I walked across the street to the Fairmont Hotel when I was representing Mayor Alioto at a meeting of mayors. Michael never expected recognition for what he did. His reward was my happiness.

Our first year we took a road trip in my long Ford van that would take us to Southern California where he grew up and where his older brother and his family lived. From there we would go to Marceline, Missouri where his parents grew up and from there to Wisconsin where I grew up. Two weeks before leaving, I got a call from Alice saying Dad had written several letters and torn them up. She said they would see me, but they did not want to see Michael. I said, "If you won't see Michael, you won't see me."

Michael's brother had a boyfriend in high school, but now he was married with three children and the music director of a fundamentalist church. That's gotta be the dumbest arrangement.

I had to see Eureka Springs, Arkansas because it was the sole outpost of freaks in the South. The town is divided by a gorge. One side has the largest cross in the South. Every day below the cross local players enact a passion play of Jesus' last nights with real people in costumes used for years and live animals. The play has the streets on the other side of town jam packed with yellow school busses from fundamentalist churches. The other side of the gorge had the one the remaining hot springs spas that made Eureka Springs popular in the Eighteenth Century with wealthy people from the East Coast who took the waters for health. The hillside was dotted with shops selling tie-died T-shirts and charming Victorian homes.

We parked the van in campsite just outside of town. As soon

as I realized we were in enemy territory, I put country music on the tape player and opened the doors of the van. Whatever objections the Arkansas families with children had for two men traveling together were put to rest when a man asked Michael where we were coming from. He told them California. The word California was all it took to put their minds to rest because it captured a wide range of craziness.

Saturday night, Michael and I danced together at the big dance party in the hotel. Michael knew one of the owners. This was 1976, and we got stares, but no one slashed my tires.

Stepbrother Woody offered us a platform in the woods on his property. Alice called him and said they would see both of us. The hour on the screen porch at Point O Pines, their summer residence, was a study in civility. Rich people have a way of being polite without scintilla of emotion, but neither of them asked what his father did. I said nothing when Michael talked about how Masonite desecrating the land he built his cabin on. I watched Dad's face because he'd been a member of the board of directors of Masonite Corporation. His face showed nothing, and Michael held his own. I went back to Wausau twice. I didn't take Michael because they embarrassed me.

John Coates was the CEO of Masonite Corporation, and he was Dad's model businessperson. I met Cappy Coates at Peter Adair's studio. Peter made one of the first gay documentaries Word is Out. I told Cappy to tell her father about me, and I would tell Dad about her. I figured, if Dad's hero had a queer kid, it would be easier for Dad to accept his queer kid.

Michael went all out for the two disco parties with seventy guests. At the first party, he turned the front parlor into a dance hall, hanging a mirrored disco ball from the ceiling, and lining the bay window frames with little white lights. A DJ friend make dance tapes for the party. The building is two and a half feet wider than the rest of the buildings on the block, and that night we needed that extra room when the men in jeans and flannel shirts, shirtless and leather vests started dancing.

He turned the shower room into the bar. One trash can was ice and beer. Another was trash. He put a board across the door that served as the bar and a bedside table beside it had liquor bottles and a stack of red cups. At the second party, he made the dining room the dance floor, hanging speakers from the four corners of the coffered ceiling. At both parties, a room was set aside with sex, and for the second party, to remind men of the mazes at the baths, guests had to navigate a closet that opened into adjacent bedrooms. At the second party, Michael rushed up to me. "You got to see them!" That was the last thing I expected from him, but he was caught up in the party's energy. By time I got to the sex room, the men had finished having sex, and they were cleaning up using paper towels and moist towelettes. Both parties had stock pots of punch on the grill of the commercial range, one clearly labeled Acid Punch.

At both parties, the long hall that ran the length of the flat was lined with some of the hottest men in town. They were our family, and if we gave them a night they remembered Michael and I had done our job.

Some of my fondest memories are the dinner parties that Michael took days to plan. The dining room with a complex coffered ceiling and wood paneling was the most elegant room in the flat. It reminded me of the Quarles home in Milwaukee. I furnished it with a Belgian arts and crafts dinner set that I found in an antique store in Berkeley. The set included a table, eight chairs, and two sideboards. I inherited Mom's sterling and a set of her fine English China with scalloped edges. He chose the main course and using Mom's silver bowls and platters and her fine china, the dinners were always elegant. For one he soaked a pork butt in milk overnight, and for another, he infused a leg of lamb with garlic and raisins. When we hosted the Wisconsin delegation to the 1984 Democratic Convention, he poached an entire salmon and covered it with thinly sliced scales of cucumber. Halfway through the evening the governor was in the flat below drinking beer and I see that half of the salmon has been eaten. While I run to get Michael, a large Wisconsin woman picks it up and flips it on the other side.

Michael spent the day in the kitchen assembling everything he needed, and I made mad dashes to retrieve the spice or the color that he missed. I was banned from the kitchen. An hour before the guests arrived, we were going crazy making sure everything was exactly right.

Eight people was the right number of guests in that room, and I selected guests I thought made for lively dinner conversation. With drinks before dinner and wine at dinner, the convivial evenings always involved spirited conversations and some stupidity. Our dinners were a gay Algonquin Round Table.

He had never seen Europe, and I wanted to show him the London I loved and Venice a world treasure. As a Christmas gift, Michael gave me a trip from London to Venice on the Orient Express. Sitting next to him in matching regally upholstered armchairs as we dined on clear broth on our way to the coast, I was an Edwardian gentleman. Somewhere in France, we went all out in tuxedoes, little black ties, cummerbunds, the whole shooting match for dinner of French delicacies and fine wine. Crossing the Alps into Italy, I was so excited I barely slept.

Michael had a sense for restaurants, and he was 99% accurate in telling from the outside that a restaurant made outstanding dishes he wanted to sample. Our first evening in Florence, the maître de in a tuxedo jacket who looked like he had been at the restaurant since beginning there as a teenage dishwasher, graciously sat us in street clothes discreetly off to the side. There, we could enjoy our meal with full service, without disturbing the rest of the diners in fine Italian evening wear. The menu was in Italian. My two years of high school Latin helped me decipher some of the entrees, but Michael ordered blind. His meal was the most delicious either of us had ever tasted, and even he couldn't decide what it was. As I was leaving baffled, I asked our waiter what Michael's dish was. In his best English he said it was liver and onions. I have seen it on menus, but it's never been the same.

Everywhere we traveled, men stopped Michael remembering how they loved being treated by him at Toad Hall. We were sometimes mistaken for brothers.

I kept what I did between eight and five in Civic Center out of our life in the flat because my time with Michael was sacred. My greatest regret is asking Michael to keep his landscaping business out of our dinner table conversations. I should have been there for him when he needed me because he was just starting the business.

Michael's good looks and his authenticity made him a charmer. I was mugged and left for dead at the corner of our block. I made it to the bottom of the stairs, but I had no keys, and I did not remember that I had been mugged. I rang the bell, and as I climbed the stairs, I told Michael that I had a terrible headache, and I needed an aspirin. Once I got to the top I got in bed, and Michael gave me two aspirin.

He had no health insurance, and the only doctor he knew was a Toad Hall regular. The Universe provided. He kept the doctor's phone number and knew where to find it. The doctor was home when he called. After explaining what happened to me, he told Michael to take me to the Emergency Room immediately. If he had not done that, I would be dead.

At Kaiser Redwood City because Kaiser neurosurgeons collaborated with their counterparts at Stanford, they drilled a hole in my skull to release the fluid gathering on my brain. I was unconscious for four days. The hospital rigidly enforced visiting hours, but when charmer Michael said that he was my man, he remained at my side for four days, only going into the city for a change of clothes.

I had just come to, and I had to pee. I hate bedpans, so I started getting up, pulling the tubes from the back of my hand. Dad who had flown in from Aspen, put his hands on my shoulders. "This is your father. The doctors want you to rest."

I replied, "I don't care who the fuck you are, I have to pee." Dad had a nurse find Michael who was having lunch. He talked me into using the bedpan. I severed the umbilical cord with Dad that day, and he knew that the most important person in my life was no longer him but Michael.

Our first year we took a road trip in my long Ford van that would take us to Southern California where he grew up and where his older brother and his family lived. From there we would go to Marceline, Missouri where his parents grew up and from there to Wisconsin where I grew up. Two weeks before leaving, I got a call from Alice saying Dad had written several letters and torn them up. She said they would see me, but they did not want to see Michael. I said, "If you won't see Michael, you won't see me."

Michael's brother had a boyfriend in high school, but now he was married with three children and the music director of a fundamentalist church. That's suicidal.

I had to see Eureka Springs, Arkansas because it was the sole outpost of freaks in the South. The town is divided along a gorge. One side has the largest cross in the South. Every day below the cross local players enact a passion play of Jesus' last nights with real people and live animals. The play has the streets on the other side of town congested with yellow school busses from fundamentalist churches throughout the South. The other side of the gorge had the one the remaining hot springs spas that made Eureka Springs popular in the Eighteenth Century with wealthy people from the East Coast who took the waters for health. The hillside was dotted with shops selling tie-died T-shirts and charming Victorian homes.

We parked the van in campsite just outside of town. As soon as I realized we were in enemy territory, I put country music on the tape player and opened the doors of the van. Whatever objections the Arkansas families with children had for two men traveling together were put to rest when a man asked Michael where we were coming from. He told them California. The word California was all it took to put their minds to rest because California captured the full spectrum of craziness.

Saturday night, Michael knew one of the owners of the hotel, and he and I danced together at the big dance party in the hotel. This was 1976, and we got stares, but no one slashed my tires.

When we got to Wisconsin, stepbrother Woody offered us a platform in the woods on his property up north. Alice called him and said they would see both of us. The hour on the screen porch at Point O Pines, their summer residence, was a study in civility. Rich people have a way of being polite without scintilla of emotion. Neither of them asked what his father did for a living. I said nothing when Michael talked about Masonite desecrating the land he built his cabin on. I watched Dad's face because he'd been a member of the board of directors of Masonite Corporation. His face showed nothing, and Michael held his own. I went back to Wausau twice. I didn't take Michael because I wanted to spare him their passive aggression.

John Coates was the CEO of Masonite Corporation, and Dad couldn't say enough good things about him. I met Cappy Coates at Peter Adair's studio. Peter made one of the first gay documentaries Word is Out. I told Cappy to tell her father about me, and I would tell Dad about her. I figured, if Dad's hero had a queer kid, it would be easier for Dad to accept his queer kid.

Michael and I dealt with my promiscuity for eighteen years. We agreed at the beginning that ours would be an open relationship. Our sex life was active the entire time. He came out blowing men on the Pier in Long Beach, so with me he worked out his sexual needs in the arcades in the dirty bookstores South of Market. I came out sexually getting boy to strip down to their white cotton underwear, so I worked out my sexual needs by having sex with friends and soon to be friends. We agreed to be home by midnight. We experimented with talking about what we did and not talking about what we did. Mostly, we played it as it happened. We never fought. I was honest. I didn't tell him everything. but I held nothing back. I never lied. He kept what he did to himself.

I didn't know there was such a thing as unconditional love because I'd never seen it in Wausau, and the professed love I did see didn't make anyone happy. I had no reason to trust love, but I loved Michael from the moment I saw him across the bar in Toad Hall until the day he died in our flat.

I don't like the term emotional monogamy because it smacks of traditional marriage. What Michael and I had was made by us for us. I didn't care what it looked like to others because it was ours. I loved him one hundred percent of the time but telling him that wasn't the most convincing argument when I was playing around. The most remarkable part of the story of my promiscuity is the way Michael dealt with it. He had the soul of an angel, and his love was unconditional. I'm embarrassed I couldn't love him unconditionally, but something in his composition allowed him to love me unconditionally and I am forever grateful.

He didn't have my passion for politics, but the times I saw him cry were when the rainbow flag the was raised the first time and whenever he heard the San Francisco Gay Men's chorus sing "San Francisco" in the Castro Theater.

Michael was diagnosed with AIDS in 1993. To hide his KS lesions, Michael designed a tattoo for his shoulder and side. The tattoo was made of yellow Japanese chrysanthemums, green vines entwined with little blue and yellow flowers, and bold black Javanese swords. He had them done by Lyle Tuttle who did the tattoos for the Hells Angels. I wasn't a fan of tattoos, but his were gorgeous.

Just as he made my life the best it could be, he didn't want to burden me when he got sick. He kept working until his crew made him to stop. He spent three weeks in hospital. Without telling me, our Kaiser doc had him transferred to a miserable care facility. It was the only facility Kaiser was willing to pay for that provided the physical therapy he needed to revive muscles that had atrophied in hospital. I'd never seen anything more depressing; it had all the joy of a morgue.

I got there one night, and Michael's eyes were bright, his

spirits were high, and he wanted to eat. I hadn't seen him like that for years, and I was deliriously excited. He was going to live, and I was jumping with joy. After months of things not getting better, he had finally turned the corner, and once again, I would have him next to me in bed when I woke. I was beside myself with happiness. This was what I'd been hoping to see.

I watched excited as he put the spoon of pudding to his lips. He put it in his mouth and smiling at his accomplishment. I knew was going to live

There was no way he could stop the pudding that dribbled uncontrolled from the side of his mouth. I'd never seen sadder eyes. That broke his spirit.

The next day, he said he was learning to live on morphine with dignity which was his way of saying he was learning to live with death with dignity. I had tears in my eyes. He wanted to come home, and after learning how to walk four steps with a physical therapist, he came home on stretcher.

Every day, I looked for a sign that Michael's health had improved. Not seeing one didn't dimmish my conviction the next day. He was strong enough, and I was convinced that he got enough rest he would get the best of HIV. Because he loved food, I focused on him eating properly, giving him something new to eat every day. Despite my best efforts, he ate little.

Michael's final gift and further evidence of this style was the fiftieth birthday party he planned for me at the John Pence Gallery on Post Street. He planned it months in advance as a surprise, but when he was unable to address the eighty invitations he had printed, he told me. Sherry Thomas my righthand on the Library Campaign and her partner Lynn Witt wrote them for him. The John Pence Gallery featured outstanding examples of realist art, my favorite style of art.

In the various rooms of the gallery each painting and piece of sculpture was perfectly lit so it glowed against the elegant dark color of the wall. The gallery exuded calm and beauty.

The guest list included Dad and Alice, Martin Paley, John Jacobs, president of the Chamber of Commerce, and the civic leaders I worked with on the library campaign. There were members of the group of the gay community's best and brightest organized by Jerry Berg in response to Prop 6. Eric Larsen and I walked to high school with, and his wife Sevim. He and I ran a Tastee Freeze one summer in Wausau. The rest were people that Michael culled from my Rolodex.

Michael's friend Rochelle catered the party. The food included some of my favorites like her eggplant caponata. My birthday cake was a carrot cake, my favorite that she smothered with thick cream cheese and confectioners' sugar frosting.

The week before the party I vacillated between finding the right red fabric to wrap his body in and trying to find a chaise lounge, so he had a place to lie and enjoy the party he planned for the man he loved.

I didn't want him to die. I couldn't live without him. I held on to that until I heard the death rattle. I called Rochelle who'd spent the afternoon with him. She got out of a soaking tub in the Oakland Hills. Todd Menard who'd been my masseur showed up unannounced with soft music tapes and candles. Sherry Thomas and Lynn Witt wanted to participate in an AIDS death. They kept telling me I was out of toilet paper, but I was frozen and did nothing. His last words to me were. "I love you." Around three AM, Rochelle told me to leave the room because if I stayed, he would want to take care of me. For half an hour I distracted myself with an ad for mattresses in the New York Times. He died at three forty AM, February 27, 1964.

Sherry Rochelle and I decided to go ahead with the party.

At the entrance to the gallery, I placed a photograph of Michael and a statement announcing his death. I only saw one person who saw it and left.

The party was bittersweet. I was so preoccupied with multiple feelings of rage, sadness, and despair I didn't eat any of Rochelle's fabulous food. At some times during the party, I was caring for the grieving more than they were caring for me. Near the conclusion of the party, Dad surprised everyone with an animated story of me being born in a snowstorm. Because that was so unlike him, Sevin Larsen remembers that every time I see her. Others shared their thoughts that touched me. After most of the guests had left, a group of closest friends formed a circle holding hands in a back gallery and we remembered Michael in silence.

Michael was one of a kind and he continues to be part of me.

He was also a private person. He greatest source of strength were his memories of his mother. She was a genius with food, and to him, she was light, air and sustenance. She was constant, never having an affair with another memory when he was out of the room. She was always there for him when he needed her. He could count on her. The kitchen was his laboratory where with her over his shoulder he communed with the food gods. He planned every dinner around her recipes as he shopped for food after his day shift at Toad Hall ended, so I never ate the same thing twice. He was always experimenting, and only once did his meal flop. I have never eaten so well. He collaborated with Rochelle who shared her Sicilian recipes and cooking techniques. I credit much of my longevity to him because since he died, I've been feeding myself using what I learned watching him.

His plating was so spectacular that Don Sagramoso who designed photo shoots for major department stores told him he should do a coffee table book of his plating.

I was honored to carry the mortgage so he could start his landscaping business. He began alone with a VW pickup, a lawnmower and assorted garden tools. When he died, he had a staff of three, two tan Toyota pickups and the black Toyota 4Runner I gave him. He had no professional training; he was natural with the earth. The showhouse in the East Bay was his first chance to make a public statement as a landscaper. Women who lunch needed something to do, so they found someone willing to donate their large home and grounds for a couple of months. During that time, designers and decorators took one of the rooms and they use it as a showcase of their talents. No one got paid, they did it for the publicity. Once the designer's wet dream was open to the public the proceeds from the ticket sales went to a women's shelter. His work there launched his career. From then on, he had constant work from wealthy families in the East Bay who wanted their garden to be a showpiece, their garden was part of their presentation to the world that announced they had refined taste and the money to pay for it. Michael knew how a plant wanted to be seen by its admiring public and how to make a plant look like it was exactly where it is supposed to be.

He made the second largest bedroom in our flat his studio. He painted the eleven-foot walls and coved ceiling a deep hearty red. His drawing table took up most of the long wall. A large wooden box held rolled up copies of his designs. He hated doing payroll, but the rest of the time he was in his element. His designs were original. Nothing flashy, plantings that looked natural. He knew how to draw your eye through a garden. There was always something you didn't expect but it felt perfectly in place. He wasn't afraid of tricking the eye. He drove all over town to collect enough of them, and he filled a field at the back of a showhouse property with thousands of plastic daffodils because the real ones don't keep their bloom. From the distance they looked real.

I could always find him at a showhouse because he would be in the center of a group anxious for his tips. He was not going to be intimidated by the landscapers with university degrees who rattled off the scientific names of plants to impress prospective clients. He took the plant identification class at State, and he aced the final exam.

Jim Hormel asked him to design and install a garden at his home on Buena Vista Terrace. The property is on a hill, so his garden is a series of graceful terraces with stone steps that seamlessly connect them. He built a deck around the giant oak. Jim was delighted, and he told me his favorites respite was sitting on the deck in the shade of the oak.

I held his memorial service in Jim's garden. Jim's gift to the National AIDS Memorial Grove got Michael's name close the center of the Grove's circle of friends right where he belongs.

He comes back to me in dreams. Six months after he died, we are walking up the Castro Street hill. He stops in front of a white Victorian. I know this is the last time I'm going to see him. I see fit men in short white towels behind the open front door. He blows me a kiss before disappearing into the bathhouse.

Then I see him on Castro Street. He's in the line to get into Toad Hall. He's with a man and he wants me to leave him alone.

Years later I am sitting next to him in the front seat of his Ford 150. He's silent, but I can feel his leg next to me. I tell him how nice it is to be with him.

In the most recent dream, we are doing something together and we talk and act the way we always did. I touch him as much as I can because I haven't felt him for years, and he's so real, I'm surprised when he disappears.

He'll always be with me.

Bars and Baths

In a city of strangers, the bars scared me at first because I'd never seen men who were that comfortable with being gay. Once I knew how to cruise, the bars were the heartbeat of the community because my generation was creating a magical neighborhood that lasted four years in the bars. They were the sun that the rest of the neighborhood orbited around.

With a Mediterranean climate I wore work clothes during the day, and I wore a leather jacket when I went to the bars at night. I lived the heyday of gay bars in San Francisco when there were twenty-two. They specialized, so I had a lot to choose from depending on my mood that night. They were where I met men I took home and had sex with, or I went home with them and had sex with. Most men had homes, so there wasn't much sex in bars. Men with different tastes and ethnicities found comfortable bars in bars that catered to them, and every pride brought us together as a rainbow community.

The bars were our Grand Central Station, a hectic meeting place, and the best place for queer information. They were the only place we could meet each other and be gay. My generation got to know each other, and we taught each other what it means to be a gay man in the bars. No one bothered us. Our culture was written on bathroom walls.

The Castro we know today, started with Toad Hall, now part of Walgreens. It was so popular, the line on Sunday of customers excited to be with men like them for the first time in their life stretched around the corner and up 18th Street. Think of that for a moment. An entire generation that had not been able to be gay their entire life, gets the first chance to be gay. The closest equivalent is an atomic bomb. The explosion frees a generation that compressed its sexual urges its entire life.

The change was that powerful. Those men had been waiting ever since they knew they were gay for that moment. Now, they had it.

Toad Hal's rival up Castro Street was the Midnight Sun, and they battled it out for most popular bar for years. One year their exterior holiday ornamentations with sleigh full of elves at Toad Hall and lines of nutcrackers at the Midnight Sun put Macy's Christmas windows to shame. An interior wall of Toad Hall was covered floor to ceiling with potted poinsettias.

The owners of Twin Peaks at the corner of Market and Castro Streets, two women, had the balls to cover an exterior wall of their bar with clear window glass, the first gay bar in the country to expose its clientele to passersby.

Moby Dick on 18th Street with a giant fish tank was the bar

for when I wanted to be in the Castro, but I didn't want to be seen in the Castro. The Nothing Special lived up to its name, so I never saw the interior. Daddy's leather bar came and went, and so did I. The Pendulum around the corner on 18th Street catered to Black men and the white men who were attracted to Black men.

Toad Hall was my first gay bar. Michael opened the bar, and the Breakfast Club convened at eleven every weekday morning. The matriarch of the club, Cupcake, called everyone Helen. His well-to-do parents were aghast when they saw him in a fifties UCLA gay protest, so for as long as he never graced the threshold of their Beverly Hills home. they paid him enough to get by. With his alcohol ruined face, a scraggly beard, and his drab caftans, he was the ugliest man I'd ever seen. The rest of the club were three alcoholics around his age.

He died of alcohol poisoning, and Michael buried his ashes beneath a dogwood at his cabin.

Thursday night at the Jackhammer was red hankie night, and one night, it felt like old home week because it was Folsom Weekend. Fisters from Europe and North America were there, and I'd played with a bunch of them. I was always impressed with the number of assorted fisters who lived outside San Francisco, and it was reassuring to know I was part of a worldwide family. That night, I was the proverbial kid in a candy store.

After dark, the six blocks of deserted and vacant light industrial buildings South of Market were a leather playground. The Ramrod, the No Name, Fe-Be's with a plaster statue of *David* in a motorcycle cap, and the Stud were the stars of the night. Because it was hard to see, so the first time I was on Folsom Street, I identified a leather bar by the apron of big hog motorcycles parked in front of it. Folsom Weekend that started as a small local event became the world's largest leather event.

The Stud, my favorite, was the world's crossroads of sorted men, artists, and thinkers, and sex was just as important to them as was being themselves. They were the crème de la crème.

The first man I went home from the Stud took me to his Twin Peaks home on stilts in a restored 1950 Plymouth coupe. I had my first gay sex with him in his bedroom painted aubergine. I'd never been in a restored car, and I'd never been inside a house on stilts and aubergine was a color I had never seen, so I knew when he started taking off his clothes that I'd fallen down Alice's well.

I met Clay at the Stud on a warm September night, and I could not believe that the most handsome man in the bar wanted to make a date with me. Making a date meant he wanted to have sex with me. He was half English and half Italian. Tall and slender with smooth Italian skin and the rugged facial features of a Saxon warrior. His long dark hair was unkempt; he was not concerned with appearances.

He was the first man who wanted to touch me. As we fooled around on his waterbed like little kids I learned to respect myself. Lying wrapped in each other on his undulating waterbed, I was open to him and his world. All the years I repressed sex, I thought about what I expected from being touched by a gay man, so given the chance to claim it, I was an open field.

He was a native San Franciscan, and with him as my guide, I found parts of San Francisco like the alleys in Chinatown that I would have never found on my own. Our first picnic was in the Presidio cemetery. As I hate the egg salad sandwich he made for me, I watched a passing ship. I ate my first pirogue with him in a Russian bakery in the Richmond.

He was authentic, he was the real deal.

Touching was complicated because being touched for gay men came with a web of highly charged emotions and a lifetime of being told that touching a man is bad. What triggers those emotions remains one of the great mysteries of life. The smartest way for me to deal with the taboos was for me to be me.

Authenticity at first was tricky because I was used to second guessing every decision like a crazy person. Once I accepted that I am sexual and that I want to be touched, I was authentic, and that attracted authentic men.

Bartenders were rock stars, and Michael was nominated for the Golden Didleaux Award as Bartender of the Year. He always had the answer when a tourist asked how to get to Golden Gate Park or where one could buy a douche hose.

I developed a routine. I went to the bars at nine. With three beers I was ready to approach a man. I was impatient, so I often initiated the conversation. I'm a fast learner, and when there's a will there's a way. I had sex every night, either at my apartment or

I made mistakes. I did wake and wonder what did I see in him, but when I saw him on the street, I acknowledged him. We were in this together.

I could never predict if the bar was going to be fun. It depended on the mood of the bartender, the music and things that can't be explained. I knew by ten-thirty if the night was going to be one of those nights were everything happens magically. I lived for those nights.

I started my night of cruising at Toad Hall. It was too tame for me, but it was a cultural icon. That meant Toad Hall was the first bar men from out of town went to on their first night in Mecca, so there was always the chance I'd see a new face. If I didn't find someone who wanted to have sex, I went South of Market, sometimes stopping halfway at The Rainbow Cattle Company. It was a laidback hippie-cowboy boots and flannel shirt bar. Men who'd moved to Sonoma County used it when they were in the city.

The Stud was a crossroads of assorted men from around the world, and it was my home for four years. I was invited to the bar's private holiday party, and when I entered in the back door, I was given tab of acid. Half the bar was carpeted with Oriental carpets, upholstered armchairs, and couches that looked like a Christmas living room. The walls in the other half were covered with blue paper that looked like ice, and mylar icicles suspended from the ceiling made it look like a Christmas wonderland.

A gorgeous man I saw in the bars but was afraid to talk to was there. Men that beautiful, to survive, protect themselves with invisible shields. I thought I could never break through a shield, so I stopped wasting my time. I was surprised when he said he wanted to come home with me.

You can't tell a man by his cover because when we got home, he was a sloppy bottom. I try to be an equal opportunity player, but sloppy bottoms disgust me.

The first time I encountered the three tall men in opera stockings, glittered beards, and platform boots at the Stud, they crossed too many lines. From a distance, I liked the idea of genderfuck because they were walking billboards declaring "I don't give a flying fuck what you think." They were also groundbreakers who dared go where gay men feared to go.

The Ambush was a dope smoking, laidback bar, and. Michael and I stopped there the nights we came back from a weekend at his cabin. One night, the man next me on a bench got fisted by a man on the floor.

A lesson in appearance versus substance was a road trip to Laguna Beach my second year out. There were four of us. A. was the ringleader who went there all the time and was its loudest cheerleader. B. was smaller and not as attractive, and he took his cues from A. The third, John, and the only one I knew before the trip, was the epitome of male beauty. His proportions were perfect, and his Northern European skin flawless. He wasn't a big man, but his smooth muscles in just the right places more than made up for it, and this was before Nautilus equipment, protein shakes and routines that have become assembly lines for six pack abs. I don't remember how I got roped into the road trip, but I was always up for a road trip, especially one with him.

We drove down Friday night and checked into our motel around midnight. The next morning A was ready to go. He knew the perfect place for a light breakfast that he timed precisely, so we could be on the beach at the right time. The beach was a mass of men who there to show off the result of hours spent in the gym and a scrupulous diet.

The minute John took off his tank top, all eyes turned on him. Past noon my skin was on fire, and when John got down to a Speedo, the game was over. I didn't have a chance meeting any man on the beach.

By the time we left the beach, I was insignificant and ugly. No one was looking at me. I'd been stage scenery that no one would miss if I weren't there.

My dinner was a Cobb salad at classy café on the water. By the time we got in the car to drive an hour to LA so that we could go to another of A.'s must-sees, an LA disco, I was wishing I'd never come. Under the flashing lights in a warehouse packed with men who worked at being gorgeous, I didn't matter and

I didn't fit in. I never went to discos because they were a lousy place to pick up men.

The other three didn't hook up, so we drove back to Laguna Beach. A. wanted to make a last-ditch effort at the Little Shrimp bar.

I got lost in the older crowd, and when I was gazing at the sea, a man said he was lonely and would I come back to his motel room with him? I was thirty, he was in his early forties and in decent shape. His reddish-brown hair was cut short, and the same color beard and mustache were professionally trimmed. His face was square, his eyes brown with just enough hair on his broad freckled chest.

He told me he was a cinematographer, and he was about to shoot the movie Shampoo with Warren Beatty and Goldie Hawn. He was generous sexually, ferocious as a bottom, and he knew how to make my ass sing He treated me as an adult. The whole time we had sex we used pharmaceutical poppers; the bullets wrapped in string. The high from them was pure and strong. They kept us going 'til dawn.

Pharmaceutical poppers are illegal in the States, and in those days, it was mark of gay manhood to make a run to Tijuana, Mexico and going from farmacia to farmacia buying a ready supply of pharmaceutical poppers.

On the ride back to San Francisco, John had an excuse for not going home with someone and the others were impressed that I spent the night with a man. What started with me feeling ugly and not as hot a John ended with me the winner.

Public Service

National LGBTQ Politics

Jerry Berg was an attorney and a visionary who knew before anyone that for the queer community to survive long term it had to have the social services that the rest takes for granted. Jim Hormel was heir to the Hormel meat fortune and a philanthropist. They along with Steve Endean, an early queer activist in Washington, DC who recognized the need for a powerful presence in Congress gave birth to the Human Rights Campaign Fund in 1980.

I was honored when Jim asked me to replace him on the nascent HRCF board in 1983. Dianne Feinstein, my boss, was the scheduled keynote speaker at the 1982 HRCF dinner in New York. On the plane to New York, she learned that she'd been disinvited because she vetoed the domestic partner bill passed by the Board of Supervisors. That's the set up for my time with HRCF.

When I told Mayor Dianne Feinstein, now a senior member of Congress, I joined the HRCF Board, she stood behind her desk unflappable. Politicians never forget those that cross them, and I paid for it later when she chose a female equivalent to be her go-to contact with AIDS. I was hurt, but let it pass because I was a damn good civil servant, and I didn't hunger for politics.

My first HRCF board meeting was a "gay friendly" concrete block hotel in Miami Beach. My immersion in queer South Florida in 1984 began with a swimming pool of Speedo junk. was used to protests marches, so that didn't sit well. I also didn't like the well-groomed hustlers who suckered drunks in elastic waist pants into paying them for their company. They were deluded into thinking that the smile of the blond boy hustler was going to make his miserable life like his life was when his father hoisted him on his shoulder so he could watch the brass band in the 4th of July parade on Main Street.

I watched disgusted when a fifty-year-old board member, well into his booze, was led like a trained seal out of the room by an eighteen-year-old in a tank top. Has he no shame? I expected better from a board member of HRCF, and I hoped I wasn't the only man on the board like me.

When I joined the board in 1982, queer people were a despised minority by most Americans. The Roman Catholic Church was a serious contender for most homophobic, and most people believed I was a mistake because men are supposed to be straight.

Queers had no visibility nationally, and politicians considered us election poison, so none would touch our money. It would be six years before Roberta Achtenberg was the first elected to the San Francisco Board of Supervisors, the first queer person elected to a public office.

In 1983 HRCF was a four-person, shoestring operation hidden in the vast sprawl of our nation's capital. Political movements passed over us never knowing we were there. HRCF not only had to break through the silence, but we had to operate like a full-scale political operation.

Political Action Committees were new, so their impact on the political process was too limited to be measured. But because they had money, corporations with lots of money quickly saw them as a way to make more money. Then labor unions got into the game.

It was bold to start at the federal level when the local level was easier, but Jerry Jim and Steve saw the need at the federal level. It was the nest step in claiming our civil rights.

I remember little of my first HRCF board meeting in that ridiculous Miami Beach hotel because I felt outclassed by my fellow board members who had more on the ground political experience than I did; one was on speaking terms with a member of congress. I didn't yet know their vocabulary, so I listened intently and watched the group's dynamics.

My introduction to national politics was watching the 1950 Democratic National Convention on the tiny screen of the television set in a room my grandparent's called the Quarters in their home on North Shepard Avenue. I was sprawled on a porte cochere with a bowl of plums until the wee hours because it took three ballots. The final contestants were Adlai Stevenson, Illinois Governor, Estes Kefauver, Tennessee Senator and Richard Russell, Jr. Georgia Senator. I knew nothing about federal politics aside from scumbag Joseph McCarthy, so I rooted for the underdog, Russell not knowing he was an arch segregationist. Adlai Stevenson won the nomination and lost to returning war hero Dwight D. Eisenhower. San Francisco is the toughest training ground for politicians because it has the highest number of politicians that end up in federal office than any city in the state: Senator Dianne Feinstein, Nancy Pelosi, Speaker of the House of Representative and Vice President Kamala Harris, former SF District Attorney.

I wanted to create change, but I'm a thinker and a visionary, so I left the down and dirty part of politics to those who do that exceptionally well. I sat in on a meeting of a San Francisco gay democratic club, and they spent an inordinate amount comparing their club to the other gay democratic club. I don't have the temperament for that. I think big, and the federal level is a better fit.

I was impressed with the board co-chairs. Duke Comegys, a casually, expensively dressed fit man from Los Angeles who raised tons of money for the Gay and Lesbian Center in LA. and Vivian Shapiro, casually dressed lesbian, who was a power in New York City politics. She helped organize the protest at the CDC.

That Sunday, I came face to face with what I was up against. Vic Basile, the executive director, convinced a retired couple into opening their home in Fort Lauderdale on a Sunday afternoon so he could introduce HRCF to South Florida. Enticed by cocktails and pool boys, the couple assembled a group of middle-aged men in Bermuda short and short sleeve shirts, and blond boys in Speedos in their cane living room. Bottles of expensive alcohol waited to be opened on an Edwardian tea table.

Duke and Vivian described the mission of HRCF, and the value of a political action committee. Vic told them how to join HRCF. One attendee in a powder blue jump suit summed it up. "What you do is so important." That queen wasn't about to lift a manicured finger. He was perfectly happy letting someone else fulfill his responsibility as member of the queer community. I was outraged.

He and the other retirees enticed by naked men on white sand beaches moved to Florida to live someplace warmer away from where they lived. Their passivity was sad.

This was 1980, and San Francisco was ahead of other cities with queer civil rights, so I was embarrassed when Dallas, New York, and Columbus, Ohio had dinners, the principal way that HRCF raised money. With no experience with fundraising, I volunteered to do a dinner in San Francisco because I thought that's what I was supposed to do. The organization needs money so I should give money. Duh! To prepare myself for my role as board member, I took a three-day course on fundraising run by the fundraising school at Indiana University at Mills College.

I thought a dinner wouldn't be that hard. Dinners are monstrous undertakings, and Jerry Berg said he'd guide me through. He meant guide, he'll tell me what to do, and I had to do it. With Jerry every detail mattered, and every decision involved careful thought and planning.

He said I had to have a dinner chair, and he was certain that Bob Sass, a book publisher who had his foot in both the wealthy side of the community and the activist side, was the perfect choice.

Bob arrived in San Francisco in the sixties as a blond boy-faced jet fighter pilot. Single, San Francisco's A Gays, deeply closeted wealthy men, scooped him faster than catching a champaign flute from Tiffany's before it hits the floor. He was their plaything until he accepted the title of chair of the board of the Human Rights Foundation that took queer people to school because he betrayed their privacy. It would take another thirty-four years before any of them, if they lived that Along, would see an LGBTQ couple get married on the steps of City Hall.

Convincing Bob to be the dinner chair required orchestrated planning. Jerry wanted the meeting set up, so Bob felt flattered. We took Bob out to dinner at his favorite Sausalito restaurant. Jerry could be eloquent, he was also full of himself, but he was persuasive. Bob signed on, and he's been a major supporter of any project I've worked on ever since.

Next, Jerry said I needed a dinner committee to do all the legwork involved in putting on the dinner. His resourcefulness continued to amaze me because he knew a couple that just happened to have a seventy-two-foot sailboat, and he talked them into letting me use their boat. Aboard the elegant craft with dinner committee prospects that Jerry culled from his Rolodex, I was jazzed to be on such a large craft sailing the Bay, and the prospects were flattered to be there with an impressive group of young professionals. There is no greater charge than a boat when it tacks to the Windward.

I had to sell tickets to the dinner, so Jerry said I needed table captains who agreed to either buy a table of ten or sell tickets at a table of ten. Jerry pulled a closeted European high-tech wonder boy, who made a fortune understanding quartz before anyone else in Silicon Valley, from his sorting hat. To get him to agree to letting us use his home for an event required another carefully orchestrated plan. This time, we look him out to dinner at his favorite Atherton restaurant because Jerry knew he always ordered their veal parmigiana.

Over dinner, Jerry did his magic, and the tech guy agreed to let me use the pool area of his mansion in the sprawling Santa Clara County hillside with one proviso: he would not be present. The guest room of his mansion had a separate entrance, so his pay for sex date for the afternoon had a way to escape unnoticed when his guests arrived at the front door. That's a terrible way to conduct a sex life, another lie in life in the closet. It's good to be the king.

The day of the event, the sun did a magnificent job of being a warm source of energy, and the pool did its job by showing up in perfect turquoise.

I knew the young man sitting alone at the pool with curly black hair and a string of large wooden beads was a friend of Mark Leno, so I befriended him. He said he played the piano. I jumped at the chance to take advantage of his talent, and I told him if he played the piano at my dinner, I would let him in to the dinner free. Russell Kassman loaned me a Bechstein piano from his piano studio, and before he became famous, Michael Feinstein played Gershwin classics at my dinner. He also paid for his ticket.

I needed a venue, and the dinner committee's early attempts at finding the right setting for the first HRCF dinner in the city were going nowhere and time was short. I panicked. This happens in every campaign I've been involved with; something goes terribly wrong at the last minute.

Michael saved my ass when he volunteered to speak with a couple, one a designer, who had one of the early lofts South of Market. He charmed them into letting me use their home for my first HRCF dinner.

Their loft of gray and black industrial design and warm wood English country furniture was a decorator's wet dream, a fantastic place for my first HRCF dinner. It was also a two-for because it sat atop Taste Catering, one of the finest caterers in town. The gay man that ran Taste Catering gave me a break on the cost of the catering. This is where things were going crazy because everything I needed was falling into my lap.

The dinner was an enormous success. It made money for HRCF, and I'd do it again just to watch the two lesbians in little black dresses and heels as they left the dinner.

This was before AIDS, and the community was just forming, so no one did fundraising dinners. The one I did with Bob was the first, and it set the bar for every dinner since. Sadly, few that I attended lived up to it.

I went to dinners to catch up with friends and eat a decent meal; they shouldn't bore me. I stopped going to one nonprofits' dinner because the ED didn't know when to stop. I thought my money was better spent elsewhere

The HRCF board met four times a year, each time in a different city to expand the base. At my board meeting at a tennis resort in Palm Springs, Vic Basile, the ED, took me aside and told me Duke was leaving the board, and both he and Duke wanted me to replace him

I was stunned. I thought my fellow board members had more hardcore political experience than I had, but they believed I could do it. I asked Duke what I should do, he said, "Do whatever Vic tells you to do." My co-chair was Hilary Rosen, now a Democratic pundit on CNN. I had the vision and the determination to keep HRCF moving ahead. Hilary was on speaking terms with members of Congress. That was critically important because at that time, elected officials feared being associated with anything queer because it would kill their chances at the next election.

During my time as co-chair of the board, HRCF spent most of its time scrambling to keep horrendous legislation from Senator Jesse Helms and similar haters from passing restrictive legislation. Republicans from the South now exercised their positions of leadership, and we were a favorite target. It would take the Clinton Administration for HRCF, then the Human Rights Campaign, to successfully pass positive legislation and have it signed by the president.

When I joined the board, HRCF had dinners in three cities, and our budget was $260,000. When I left the board as co-chair in 1986, there were HRCF dinners in ten cities, a few federal elected officials spoke at our dinners, and we raised $2,100,000.

In 2020, the Human Rights Campaign raised $45,604,000, and any self-respecting Democrat or the few remaining moderate Republicans were fools if they failed to kiss HRC's ring.

Three Mayors

In 1968 I believed the best way to stop suffering was government. As a thinker I knew I could make the most difference drafting policy positions and designing campaign strategies as close to the center of political power as possible. Three mayors wanted to see if I had what it took to work in politics.

Joe Alioto, 1968-1971

Joe was a rising star in the Democratic Party, but thoughts of a potential presidential candidacy were squashed when Republicans falsely associated him with the Mafia.

My first job that involved the mayor was writing an application to HUD for the first federal community development money. I did it with Dean Macris, who had the uncanny ability to have a city bureaucrat who had no reason to like him and didn't want him treading on his turf, convinced by the end of the conversation that doing what Dean proposed was in his self-interest and smart politics.

Joe speed read and had a steel-trap mind, so once he understood what the grant would do for the city and his reputation as mayor, he didn't want to see anything until we presented him with the finished product. He knew I was gay, and my office was across the hall from his office in Room 200, so he couldn't miss me. Our application was successful, and the city was awarded the grant. My next job was setting up the first Mayor's Office of Community Development in the basement of City Hall. I reviewed staff choices with Dean, and I helped design the methodology for deciding which local group was eligible to receive our money.

One April afternoon, the deputy mayor, John Tolin, asked me if I liked New Orleans. I told him I did, and he said, "The Conference of Mayors is holding a conference on urban technology in New Orleans, and you are representing the mayor." I told him I didn't think I was the right person for it.

"The ticket's on your desk."

Things moved fast in the mayor's office, so there is no time to quibble, and trips like that are perks that come from working for a mayor. That trip was a ticket to me falling in love with New Orleans' decadence and making a life-long friend, Tony Masters. I quietly observed the conference sessions making intelligent observations from time to time, so I didn't come across as a complete idiot.

New Orleans is an American treasure, and that's where I spent most of my time. The wrought iron second story balconies, the boxes of oysters on a bed of ice, and the St

Charles Avenue trolley made the city a gracious wonderland. It was my second home for three months.

The conference hotel was a block from the Bourbon Pub, and that is where I met Tony Masters. I spent my second night in New Orleans in his home on Delachaise Street that Tony shared with Doug Ballard. Between the two of them, they created a masterpiece of quiet elegance. Doug had an eye for beauty and Tony had an eye for opportunities. They curated and sold the antiques crafted by artisans in England in their shop on Magazine Street. I would spend three weeks with them when I took a sabbatical in 1981. Tony was a wild man. He had the best weed and he loved anal sex. He took me on two successive days to the homes of women who'd divorced well. Both were in their early fifties, and both made up so well it looked like they didn't use makeup. They were active, and both wore individual expensive and oh so casual tasteful clothing. They each had strong weed and cold Vodka. The first listened intently to Tony talk about his friend Jerry who had just moved from one of the largest homes in the Garden District. I've seen it, and one room was entirely animalia. All the furniture and picture frames in the room were made entirely from animal bones to a grand home in the Quarter so he can be close to his high-end jewelry store on Royal Street. He described a recent bracelet Jerry bought that was first owned by Alexandra Feodorovna the last Czarina of Russia and what it cost. I was spellbound. The second woman remined me of Jane Fonda. She couldn't stand her daughter, yet they talked every day on the phone. She and Tony laughed about her affair with the husband of the wife I saw the day before. I couldn't get any closer to the truth of New Orleans decadence than those two afternoons.

George Moscone, 1975-1978

When he took office, I was still heading an office of eleven working off a grant from the regional federal departments to produce a report that detailed every federal dollar that the city in its over thirty departments and commissions received in a year. I chose the staff wisely, and I thought the report we produced, the first of its kind, was a stunning achievement.

On any given day, when a San Francisco mayor sits down at his desk in Room 200, he is confronted with at least three crises. In addition to them, there is a host of less immediate but just as important constituency issues that he must do something about just so he can get it off his desk. With all of them, the mayor makes a political calculation that involves balancing one side's interest against another side's interest and what it means to him next time he runs for office. A mayor's life is chaotic

The Clearinghouse assessment I did was something Mayor Moscone didn't asked for, so he had no personal stake in it. The large sums of money in the report did get his attention, and he used the total amount of federal money the city received in a speech when he commemorated the opening of a community health clinic. After that, I have no idea what happened to the report.

George was not mayor long. Supervisor Dan White assassinated him after less than two years in office. Everyone liked George, the good Catholic boy because who made it all the way to Room 200 City Hall, the mayor's office. George was a genuinely nice guy.

Dianne Feinstein, 1978-1988

She was a stern taskmaster who insisted that everything be done her way, and she knew more about the city than any mayor I worked with. She gave explicit instructions, but if I misunderstood the meaning of a specific word, she came down on me. She was notorious for calling staff in the middle of the night and expecting them to get out of bed and meet her wherever she was in the city. I was spared her calls because I was not gung-ho politics like most of her staff. Politics attracts a certain kind of person. They get a charge from being that close to the center of power and being able to tell their friends and family they work for a politician. With people on the lower end of the political spectrum, that means a lot. She never fired me because I performed my job better than the other staff at my level, and she knew I was there that Sunday morning she met secretly with Dean Macris and one of her political advisors to assess her chances of beating Joe Alioto in the upcoming election. I also had two ivy league degrees, so that made me in her eyes special.

My time with Dianne came to a head at a community meeting at the Valencia Rose and Josie's Cabaret & Juice Joint in the Mission because she wanted to close the baths and I wanted to keep them open. AIDS was decimating the community, and the community was torn between men like Bill Kraus, who believed closing the baths would save lives, and Michael Petrelis, an outspoken proponent of privacy in public-sex venues. I'd never seen the community so divided, and it pissed me off because the chosen people were being haters, and I wanted the honor of being haters to stick with Republicans.

Merv Silverman, the Director of Public Health, was there

to glean information from the community and to tell the community what the department was doing with AIDS. The community fought long and hard, and finally achieved their goal of having bath houses codified into city law. Activists did not want that taken away because for them the baths were a symbol of our success at claiming our right to live our way. Closing them was denying our existence.

That night, the discussion got ugly. When men were protecting a vital part of being a gay man, it laid bare their animal instincts. I'd never heard such brutal attacks on a person's integrity. Nothing was spared when it came to diminishing the enemy. What began as a heated debate turned into terrorist warfare, and I feared for my physical safety.

The meeting ended with the sides still feeling the same way. What was clear was that the community could implode any moment. Dianne reluctantly supported the bathhouse legislation because when she first ran for the Board of Supervisors, some of her supporters were gay men with money. But men having sex in a public space crossed her Catholic school girl line. She closed the baths adroitly because she closed them for health reasons without denying their importance.

Chuck Frutchey was my source of inside information on AIDS. He was a Merit Scholar who dropped out of Michigan State so he could spend a year learning how to be gay in a gay commune. He founded the Kaposi Sarcoma Foundation, now the San Francisco AIDS Foundation, and he served on the community board of the pharmaceutical giant Burroughs Wellcome. Nights were spent debating the best way to get gay men to pay attention to safe sex. My attitude around closing the baths differed from Dianne's because I thought bath houses were ideal place to disseminate safe sex information because they were ground zero. You couldn't get any closer to the men you wanted to reach. Merv Silverman thought there were good reasons to keep the bathhouses open, but he worked for the mayor. I met Chuck in the apartment he shared with Scott Smith, Harvey Milk's lover. On the back porch, we were smoking weed, and I felt his crotch, and I couldn't believe I was feeling a dick. With a gift that extraordinary, Chuck knew it would be the part of him that men would remember, and he was remarkably casual with the attention. He was one of three men I played with that had huge dicks. Men I knew reacted to giant dicks in two ways. One type saw it as a challenge, and if he succeeded, he put a notch in his belt. The greedy man makes a mess of things because his only goal is getting the monster as far down this throat as possible, while the connoisseur takes his time because he wants the experience to be enjoyable for both him and the man with the monster dick, and his reward is seeing the smile on the man's face. The other type is scared to touch it. He's never seen a dick that big and because he doesn't know his body, he's afraid it would hurt them, especially if he tried to insert his monster in his tight tender ass. Chuck's philosophy was to see what happens wrapped in his enthusiasm for sex. I call him the second Mayor of Castro Street because his daily routine started at Pasqua, now Starbucks on eighteen Street. His targets were the new men in town, and invariably that ended with his showing the man his style of San Francisco sex on the couch of his bed if they get that far. I can't tell you how many men told me Chuck was their first sex in San Francisco on the couch or his bed if they got that far.

He had a group of friends that didn't want to have sex with him They were astounded by exceptional brain, they were his big bang theory gang. They spent hours debating the meaning of sex in Michel Foucault writings about sexuality and implications of string theory.

He sold his life insurance policy, and he used some of the money to go to Australia with me. We stayed at gay owned clothing optional resort that had the only beach on the Coral Sea. When we got there, a statuesque woman lounged on a pool lounge next to the pool surrounded by gay boys in Speedos. We looked at each other, and knew we had to change that. When Chuck dropped his towel, the mood changed, and by the time it was time to go in for dinner, most of the men had discarded their Speedos. Chuck established a hot tub ritual. Before dinner he would get in the hot tub, and he'd have sex with a man by dinner time. It was so constant that by our last day men joked about it. I envied his ability to strike up a conversation with a stranger.

Our affair lasted four months. Michael knew about it, and when he asked me to stop having sex with Chuck, I stopped.

David Wharton, a gay man, asked me to run his campaign for mayor. Since he was running against Dianne, I had to do it undercover. I drew on my experience running campaigns in high school. He scared Dianne so badly; she made a much-publicized meeting surrounded by reporters and TV cameras with him in front of his home on Diamond Heights. He didn't win, but he garnered enough votes to make him a respected campaigner.

I cannot live politics 24/7 and my ego is fragile, so by the time I was working for Dianne, my job was paychecks until I could find something more rewarding.

Dirt from the mayor's office. Dianne was in a tizzy about something she'd seen. She summoned the queer people she put on city boards and commissions to her Room 200 in City Hall. Gathered around her desk, she opened the bottom drawer and pulled out a porn magazine. Knowing exactly the hard dick that got her Catholic girl school training up, she pointed to the photo, exclaiming, "You can buy that filth a block from here!"

The attendees covered their faces, but if you listen closely, you can still hear their snickers reverberating along the marble corridor outside Room 200.

Tragedy

The darkest day was the day Supervisor Dan White murdered Mayor George Moscone and Supervisor Harvey Milk, the first gay man elected to public office. He was my friend and inspiration, and he is Superman to gay men around the globe.

On May 29, 1979, I was called out of the meeting. That never happened. It was Dean Macris, my mentor. He told me supervisor White had murdered Milk and Moscone.

Michael and I joined the saddest crowd of men I'd ever seen at the intersection of Market and Castro. Quilt activist and close friend of Harvey, Cleve Jones, on a bullhorn, instructed us to walk down Market Street to City Hall peacefully. By that time, the crowd had grown beyond the intersection and masses were pouring in from the side streets. The sense of grief was a caged tiger. I was horrified at White's savagery. How could a man do that to another human being? I lost a good man who worked for change, and it would take time to process my sadness into something useful.

We were given candles as we began moving out of the intersection. Bundled in the cold, I hugged men I had not seen in years, and wherever I looked, the sadness was all-consuming. As we passed the Mint, I heard a shofar being blown, and then Joan Baez's angelic voice sang Amazing Grace." By the time I got to Civic Center, the corridor of mourners behind me stretched all the way up Market Street to Castro Street with more pouring in from side streets. That night, the queer nation mourned the death of Harvey Milk in one of the saddest displays in the city's history.

Dan White was sentenced to a maximum sentence of seven years and eight months in prison on May 21, 1979. I was in shock. The ruling smacked of favoritism; cops covering for cops. The inane sentence was too lenient. The sonovabitch that murdered George Moscone and Harvey Milk, the great hope of the community, got pat on the wrist! What the fuck was going on? It was bullshit!

I wasn't the Lone Ranger. Wave after wave of thousands of angry protestors bundled in jackets and parkas stormed Civic Center. Our progress towards full civil rights reached new heights when Harvey was elected, but White's judgment wiped it out by saying Harvey Milk's death was no different than a property owner being fined for failing to fix a ruptured pipe.

Next to a reflecting pond. I held Michael and we are mightier than a judge.

Speakers extolled Harvey and others voiced the communal outrage at District Attorney Joe Freitas, =a onetime activist with Common Cause who got a law degree. Where was the justice? This is America.

A commotion rumbled behind the makeshift stage. A glass door shattered, and yelling echoed off the Beaux-Arts buildings surrounding Civic Center Plaza. An angry mob tried to find a way into City Hall. The energy continued to build

This was the first time I was this close to a mob, and it was terrifyingly scary because it had a life of its own. Once started, it couldn't be stopped, a frightening spectacle of madness. If I got within spitting distance, I'd be sucked into the madness.

The mob could explode into violence at any moment. I was quaking in my boots. Do I go with my gut and plunge into the madness, or do I do the sensible thing and watch the mob from the safety of home?

The man who told me to come out had been murdered, and the best a jury of his peers could do was to tell the man who murdered him to sit in the corner. What the fuck was the jury thinking? Once again, a straight, white man, Joe Freitas, saved the ass of another straight white man.

I watched the psychology of the crowd. At first the mob had buoyancy because it didn't care what it did because they believed they had every right to be angry.

Cleve Jones's urging the crowd on raised the temperature and the crowd changed from buoyancy to revenge. They wanted blood! The pace of the night switched to fast forward and in a second it was out of control. A volatile group shoved me clumsily as they raced toward the center. Then another group breached my protections, and I was caught between mobs on both sides.

I tried get out of the way and I tripped and fell. I rolled over into bushes and I didn't move. When I knew it was safe, I got on a bench, and when I touched my leg, it hurt and there was blood on my hand. I took my shoe off, and the blood in my shoe spilled onto the dirt.

The complexion of the crowd changed again. The mob now had a vortex near the front of the podium. Like the particles of dust in the air, waves of anger radiated in ever widening circles. It was about to snatch me and hurl me into the vortex when I saw an opening and I walked as fast as I can through it to the periphery.

I hobbled up Fulton Street, and I was depleted when I slid the key into the lock. I made it as far as the living room and turned on the TV. Channel Seven had a line of cop cars ringing Civic Center Plaza engulfed in billowing smoke and angry flames. Civic Center Plaza was a full-scale war zone.

There wouldn't be another LBGTQ elected official until Roberta Achtenberg was elected to the Board of Supervisors ten years later in 1989.

My Fifteen Minutes

"In the future, everyone will be world-famous for 15 minutes"–
Andy Warhol

Library Story

My history with libraries began at Wausau's Carnegie library's children's library. It was ten city blocks from my home. Getting there at six, I walked from a block of timber baron, millionaire mansions to six blocks of low rent housing, an impersonal office building, an auto repair shop, and the city's premier Roman Catholic church. After crossing a busy street out of town, the gray stone library sat across the street from a WPA post office and the Nash car dealer.

I went through its collection of biographies of famous Americans, George Washington, Clara Barton, George Custer, Thomas Edison, et al. They were child-sized books, each with a frontispiece with the profile of the person's head. Then I read every book with the story of a boy who escapes the restrictions of a small town. Mom told me I could read *Tom Sawyer*, but not *Huckleberry Finn*.

In junior high, I read all the Landmark Books about famous people and events in the western world that I could get my hands on. In senior high, I had to go to the county library to find Coronel Meeks dog books, each about a different breed of dog.

The best part of Dartmouth's Baker Library was the Orozco murals. His portraits of Mexican peasants and skeleton scholars in black robes and mortarboards were the most radical statement on the cold, Puritan, New England campus, and one of the few places on campus where I felt safe.

The first time I used a card catalog was San Francisco's main library, I was married and searching for a book that would explain homosexuality to me. I started looking in the Ps, thinking a book on psychology would have what I needed, but instead the books I found were about homosexuality as a mental problem and it being dysfunctional. *What the fuck?* San Francisco had been harboring queers since the Gold Rush days, and it didn't have a book that explained homosexuality? That filled me with anger. Exasperated and feeling abandoned by the gods, I stormed out, and in my hurry, the spine of *City of Night* caught my eye. I stopped in my tracks. Making sure no one could see me, I opened the book to a scene with a hustler in a sleazy LA bar. He was not my kind of guy, but he was there in print, and that made him real. For the first time in my fucked-up life, gay men were real, not a figment of my imagination of those cold, lonely nights of perpetual winter in Wausau.

My connection with the Gay and Lesbian Center in San Francisco's New Main Library began when Martin Paley was hired as president of the San Francisco Library Foundation in 1985. The Foundation was established for the explicit purpose of raising money for the New Main Library because the activist Friends of the Library didn't have the capacity to raise large sums of money. Steve Coulter, the gay president of the Library

Commission, and Martin Paley believed fundraising for the Main Library, the most democratic city department, should reflect the city's diversity, so instead of raising money from the usual fat cats the opera and symphony hit up every year, he and Steve agreed on the concept of affinity groups, and four would represent the city's Chinese, Hispanic-Latino, African-American, and Gay and Lesbian communities.

Mom had died recently, so I volunteered the head the Gay and Lesbian Affinity Group. If an affinity group raised two hundred and fifty thousand dollars, they got naming rights for one of the library's corner reading rooms. I'd been involved in the community securing our civic rights with the Human Rights Campaign Fund, and I supported Mark Leno as he moved from County Supervisor to State Assembly, State Senate. I saw the gay and lesbian center as my chance to take the next step and take on the wealthy elite, couples like Don and Doris Fisher of The Gap and prove that my community was composed of fully functioning women and men proud of our sexuality who work at their level.

The campaign for the Hormel Gay and Lesbian Center was born on September 9, 1985, over breakfast at Zuni Café. Steve Coulter, who'd seen the Schomburg Center for African American Studies at the New York Public Library, wanted a similar center for gay people in the New Main.

We drank tea, there were no coffee drinkers among the founders of the Gay and Lesbian Center. We talked about a perfect Gay and Lesbian Center. Steve wanted cubicles that scholars used for extended periods of time. Being realistic we pared it back. By the time the bill was paid, we had a goal of $1.3 million. No gay or lesbian non-profit had ever raised that much, but no one flinched.

My campaign had a ripple effect with another affinity group. Mayor Willie Brown advised Dr. Coleman, who led the African American affinity group, that he shouldn't expect to raise more than $25,000 from the African American community, but when Dr. Coleman heard of our million-dollar goal, he raised the African American goal to the full $250,000.

Just as I got started, the Gay and Lesbian Historical Society threw up a roadblock. They didn't trust the library would always be queer friendly. A future change in city administration could mean the library got rid of its queer holdings. I doubled down, and the library committed to permanently funding a curator for the center, and the historical society agreed that any of their material that was loaned to the city met its standards for cataloguing.

I had a lot to learn in a brief period. Everyone had a library story; I wasn't the only one. Libraries were the place queer kids went in search of information to help them understand why they feel different from the other kids at school. It was almost universal. I got a letter from a woman in the Midwest who said a librarian turned her life around. Similarly, the most common complaint I heard from the founders was that when they like me were growing up, their local library didn't have books with people like them in them. That strengthened the founders' resolve that the center be a place where kids would have a place to turn when they were struggling with their sexuality.

While the Library Foundation was separate, I had to collaborate with librarians. Librarians weren't the woman with a bun in their hair who told you to be quiet; they were specialists on certain subjects; they knew how to repair a book, and the profession attracted GLBTQ people. One of them knew how to find what I needed, and he suggested books that enriched my search.

Until Google and the Internet, librarians were expected to know everything, or if they didn't know, they knew where to find it. Consequently, some librarians had a God complex. You don't get away with thinking you're smarter than me, because I am proud of my smarts, and I have nurtured them all my life; I know how much I don't know.

There was fiction between me and a group of librarians who believed raising money for the library poisoned what the library purchased. As a member of the board of KQED, San Francisco's public radio and TV station, I knew as a board member I had no right to interfere with the artistic decisions of the staff, so I let their complaint sit on my desk. When they stopped getting attention, they stopped carping.

Because libraries always have books on the shelves, I never thought about the trip that a book takes from the time the author finishes their final draft of the manuscript to when it gets on the shelf in a library. Any author will tell you, getting their final manuscript edited and picked up by a book publisher requires the patience of Job.

Every year, the library buys its books for the year based partially on the recommendations from the heads of each department of the library; some, like atlases and subscriptions, were ordered automatically every year. The back of the library where all the work is done that gets a book on a shelf is as large as the rest of the library, and no one except librarians ever sees it. Once a book gets to the back of the library, it gets catalogued to the Library of Congress standards and information about the book is put in the library's computer. Once the book is good enough to get into circulation, it is sent to the right department, and they decide where it goes on their shelves.

I always thought of libraries as local, but when I started the campaign, I discovered that libraries have been the repository of every great civilization's culture. Within the great libraries of the world are the words and the ideas of the people who made those civilizations great. They are so much more than the snapshots in a photo scrapbook; they hold the richness of a civilization's culture. The great Library of Alexandria, with the single greatest accumulation of human knowledge. was destroyed in a series of fires, and that made the Gay and Lesbian Center essential to the future of the community because if our literature is destroyed, as Hitler tried to do, we would have zero history of our culture and I have no place that holds the stories of my past.

Until recently, what was written about queer lives and their societies throughout history didn't exist. Our books and artwork were burned when a civilization went through a period of fundamentalist religion, the material it was written on dissolved over time, or a family member thought it was smut and after a queer person died, they tossed it in the trash. The Center would be the first place in the world with a mission to collect and preserve queer literary culture.

The absence of our history boggled my mind. The Center took on a whole new meaning. Being the repository of our culture made the success of the campaign even more imperative. I wasn't just making a comfortable place in a library where queer people can read books about queer people; I was building the Library of Congress of queer culture.

The other affinity groups in 1985 were Long-established communities that had gone through the Depression and the World War Two together. The head of each group sat on the Board of Directors of the Library Foundation. They weren't familiar with queer people, but they treated me as an equal.

I am quick to respond, and that set up a competition between me and Carlotta del Portillo, the woman who headed the Latino-Hispanic group. Unlike her counterparts, she was politically active. I wanted to get the work in front of me done because we had a lot of do, but she went off on tangents.

The only hostility I felt was the resentment from a rabble-rouser librarian. Being loud and determined, she was used to being the thorn in the side of library administration, but the success of the Gay and Lesbian Affinity Group surprised everyone, and that got everyone's attention, and she couldn't stand that.

I was responsible for selling a $1.3 million campaign to the community at the height of the AIDS epidemic. Every non-profit in town was scrounging for the last penny in a small pool of available funds. Before our first mail piece went out, I insisted, "I don't want a dime of anyone's money that would otherwise go to an AIDS organization." The statement appeared on every piece of literature that left the office.

I also had to keep the founders enthusiastic about an idea that never crossed their minds. As head of the team, they counted on me to provide them with reasons to support the Center because they needed those reasons when they asked their friends and associates to support the campaign. At every meeting, they would need another reason.

Since the project started books and their importance to the community fascinated me. Books are an amazing world of ideas that spawned social revolutions and protected cultures from extinction. Slovenia was part of the Roman Empire, the Ottoman Empire, Austro Hungarian Empire, the Nazi empire and finally part of the Soviet Union. Its culture was preserved in its poetry, so when Slovenia was established as a country, its history was intact. Powerful books like Karl Marx's *Das Kapital* and Thomas Paine's *Common Sense* fueled revolutions. I translated that into my first rationale for donating.

I read a story about a pope burning dirty books that piqued my imagination. Connecting it to the campaign marinated in my brain overnight. Once I had a convincing argument about the importance of preserving our culture based around that story, I had another argument for supporting the Center when I met with the founders,

I had long been curious about my gay ancestors, and I turned that into another sales pitch. With friends dying, knowing our queer ancestors was essential, because the dying needed to know they were not alone. They were part of an extensive line of historical figures like Sappho and Leonardo da Vinci. For men, whose families had disowned them, knowing that they were part of a queer family gave them a sense of belonging.

The most poignant story was the story of Magnus Hirschfeld's Institute for Sexual Research in Berlin. His was the first known collection of "sexual transitions," his term for homosexuals, transvestitism, and hermaphrodites. His books were among the first books burned by the Nazis. I used his story to remind the founders that we are a significant culture, and since most of us were not raised by queer parents, the only way our culture is passed from generation to generation is our books, therefore our literature must be preserved and protected.

Lesbian publisher Sherry Thomas, a member of the Eureka (Castro) branch library Community Advisory Committee, was hired by the Foundation, and she did an outstanding job supporting me throughout the entire campaign. I was the visionary that kept the campaign focused on our goal, and she knew a heck of a lot more about queer literature. She also knew women in Florida with a collection of lesbian literature so vast that they had to buy the house next door to store it. I worked out an annuity agreement with them, and he Center now has the country's finest collection of pulp paperbacks in the Barbara Grier and Donna McBride Collection.

Donations of a thousand dollars got the donor's name on the donor wall outside the Center on the third floor. It was the first time in history that a gay or lesbian couple could see their names together as a couple a public space. Lance Henderson suggested the 30/30 formula: thirty dollars for thirty months makes $1,000. It was wildly successful and most paid it off early.

Noted muralists Charlie Brown and Mark Evans, whose fantastic work graces hotels and public buildings around the globe, donated their services for a mural on the ceiling of the Center. The mural depicts men and women laying foundation stones, each stone has the name of a queer author. Today with its ceiling, the Hormel Center is the most visited room in the library, and all year queers bring their relatives to the donor wall to point out their name on the wall.

I asked Jim Hormel to be our lead gift with a gift of a million dollars. His gift of $500,000 included $100,000 for an endowment with the proviso that if the library lowered its support for the Center from the time it took the money, he would take his money back. That's smart philanthropy because it assured his investment would continue to benefit the community.

The opening of the Center dinner as the hottest ticket in town and not just in the queer community; everyone in town wanted a ticket. We oversold, and the Hyatt Regency had to open the foyer adjacent to the biggest ballroom that holds nine hundred people to accommodate everyone. On the day of the dinner, I couldn't speak. I gargled oceans of saltwater, and I sucked mouthfuls of lozenges to no avail. At the podium in front of a crowd excited to be finally recognized as legitimate community and a spotlight that was focused on me, my first word stuttered; but looking over a sea of my brothers and sisters who'd done so much, I formed my second word clearly, and I went with my speech about how we had been given the opportunity to show the straight world that we could do anything that they could do. When I finished, I got a standing ovation.

I raised more money than the other affinity groups, and no one had ever seen my kind of fundraising, so I was asked to speak with library fundraisers in Seattle and Fort Lauderdale, and I sat on various fundraising panels. I was given an award. At one panel, the development director of a gay non-profit in Superior, Wisconsin, told the panel about her group and their problems raising money. When she said one of their biggest supporters was a leatherman who had an elaborate dungeon, I told her to have him host a fundraising leather brunch in his dungeon. She loved the idea, and the rest were impressed with my original thinking. I was fundraising's Golden Boy.

The campaign raised $3,500,000,00 from thousands of donors with the second largest number of donors in Washington, DC.

The campaign gave the queer world its first colossal repository of its culture.

The San Francisco Library Campaign made me overnight the most popular guy in town, but I never wanted to be a celebrity.

I did not need red carpets or a fan club, and I would go crazy if paparazzi assaulted me every time I left my driveway. I put everything into the library campaign, and I needed time to unwind.

Fate had other ideas. Rick Laubscher, who spearheaded the campaign to restore the old trolleys on Market Street, asked me to be a founding governor of the City Club. What I liked about starting a project from scratch was I didn't have to conform to a tradition, no one was going to tell me, "It's always been done this way" and I wouldn't be treading on someone else's achievement. Once I started, I asked Ron questions about the purpose of the project and what I had to work with. When he answered them, he also talked about other people who'd agreed to be governors. I knew Dianne Feinstein and Jim Hormel and I recognized names from seeing them in the paper. Others were complete strangers.

From what he said, they liked the idea of the club, and they were pleased to be asked to be founding governors. I don't remember any of them ever doing anything to get the club opened, however. He used other governors for specific asks, but the rest fell to Ron and me.

The club would replace the stodgy Stock Exchange Club with a dinner club that represented all San Franciscans. The club would demolish years of dining on ordinary food in dreary rooms and replace it with a dining club that was brought back to its former Art Deco glory. I would have a top-notch chef in the heart of the business district, and it would actively solicit members from women, Asians, Blacks, Hispanics, lesbians, and gay men. The well-heeled, white corporate types who used their wealth to create massive barriers to protect them from the real world for the first time would dine with the people who made them wealthy. They were just as worthy citizens as the corporates were. Minorities were the backbone of the city that made them wealthy, and they deserved a place at the table.

Sitting at my desk, I enjoyed imagining a baron of business dining with a queer scientist, an Asian lesbian architect, and an African American who owned her own business. They looked alike as they sat freshly scrubbed and well-dressed in a landmark building, their only differences skin color and who they fucked.

Word of gay people being involved in the mainstream would spread when club members told their colleagues in cities around the world about a delightful dining experience in a club that celebrated diversity

I didn't expect street activists or our poorly paid teachers to be members of the club, but the diversity of the club was a powerful statement that, at the highest economic levels in San Francisco, queers had a place.

At the dinner celebrating the opening of the club, everyone was smartly dressed. They talked eagerly amongst each other. They were excited at being part of the club that was breaking new ground in the heart of the business district. I hadn't worked with any of them on getting the club open, so I sat next to Jim Hormel.

Next time I'm downtown, I'll drop by the club to see if my name is still next to Dianne's on the founding governor's plaque.

Save the Bay Area

The Bay Area has Long been a leader in environmental awareness thanks to the grass roots. Kay Kerr, Sylvia McLaughlin, and Esther Gulick championed open space and Bayshore restoration in the East Bay. Farmers and environmentalists in Marin and Sonoma counties formed land trusts to preserve agricultural land from speculative development. Voters in Alameda County and Contra Costa County funded the vast East Bay Regional Park District.

As Director of Planning at the Association of Bay Area Governments (ABAG), the regional land-use organization, I prepared annual reports of Bay Area growth and development. The Bay Area experienced continue intense development since the end of World War Two. The population of the Bay Area went from 2,261,300 in 1950 to 7,002,400 in 2010.

During those years, freeways were built to connect the 101 municipalities in the nine-county Bay Area.

Each municipality, through its zoning, determined its housing density and its street and highway capacity. Many mayors and city managers saw housing development as a terrific way to improve the city's tax base, so they encouraged development. Once the housing was in place, as it aged it became clear the development was putting ever greater demands on public safety, schools, and open space. City managers for the first time were asking if there would be enough water, and city engineers wondered if the existing wastewater facility could properly treat all the new wastewater. None considered how development in their city affected everyone else in the region.

I witnessed an ongoing battle between cities that understood the importance of regional government to control development and those who believed they had the right to make their own decisions. Nothing was done, and cities continued to compete for more favorable development at the cost of other cities.

I signed off on the Environmental Impact Report for every major development in the Bay Area, and I watched Petaluma enacted growth limits while in nearby Rohnert Park it ran rampant. ABAG was toothless, so there was nothing I could do about it but watch in horror.

Santa Clara County eliminated the orchards that once provided the country with most of its fruits and vegetables. Natives remembered playing in pear orchards as kids. Our reports described in detail ways that a community can grow and not harm the environment, but developers and their lobbyists in Sacramento had louder voices and more money.

Public offerings of high-tech companies made overnight

millionaires, but the people who worked in their companies could not afford Santa Clara County. They were forced to commute from as far away as Tracy and Merced in the Central Valley. Our reports kept track of the growing disparities in wealth.

San Francisco's African Americans moved to Oakland and Richmond because the housing costs were lower than housing costs in San Francisco. But Oakland and Richmond were just as dangerous because when they planned the redevelopment areas in San Francisco's Hunters Point and the Western Addition, officials ignored the community's underlying problem of poverty.

Future regional government better face address racial justice, or Black Lives are going matter in an even bigger and uglier ways.

To reign in growth in the Bay Area and make it sustainable, Joe Bodovitz, who headed the first Bay Conservation Development Commission and the California Coastal Commission, wanted to merge the regional land-use agency ABAG, the Association of Bay Area Governments, and MTA, the regional transportation agency, into a single regional government. The State would have to enact legislation. Joe hired me to convene a group of business leaders and environmentalists and draft state legislation for a Bay Area regional government while he took care of the politics. He hired me to help him, and the first thing I did was head hunting.

I spent a month scrutinizing a pile of seventy resumes. I was looking for clues that someone would be interested in an idea that they didn't know was important to them, regional government. Because there hadn't been one, they didn't know what I was talking about, so my sales pitch had to include something that had value to them. Then it wasn't safe to admit I was gay. Once someone looked promising, I called their references. By the end of the month, I had twenty mostly white, civic-minded men. Joe and I decided the best person to lead the group was an eager young man who ran KPIX, the local CBS station and wanted to make his mark with the city's power elite.

At our first meeting, they identified the three key issues: transportation, housing, and environmental protection. They broke up into teams, and worked up papers on the current situation and ramifications of certain decisions for the future of the Bay Area.

While they were doing that, I collaborated with a gay Assembly staff member on drafting legislation. Referencing existing legislation and what I could learn from the DC regional government, I wrote state legislation. My proposed legislation was emailed back and forth until we had wording that balanced jobs and the environment and had the best chance of passing the State Assembly and Senate.

I had to balance multiple interests and their impact on each other in a dance of compromise and second-guessing politicians,

Joe said my work saved him the cost of an attorney.

Willie Brown, then the powerhouse in the State Assembly, was on board. Republican Governor Peter Wilson was inclined to support our bill if there was sufficient popular support. Quentin Kopp, a persnickety former San Francisco Supervisor and then state Senator, nixed the deal because he'd been on the MTA Board, and he didn't want their power diminished, plus he was a jerk.

All the arduous work that Joe, I, and committed leaders put into a sound proposal for regional government was flushed by a frustrated white man.

Regional government is more than transportation and land use; it's clean air and water and it is rebuilding public utilities, so they aren't taken out of service by an earthquake. The need is urgent, and climate change is making things worse, so regional government will keep coming back. Without it, some of next Bay Area generation will be swimming to school.

The darkest day was the day Supervisor Dan White murdered Mayor George Moscone and Supervisor Harvey Milk, the first gay man elected to public office. He was my friend and inspiration, and he still is Superman to gay men around the globe.

On May 29, 1979, I was called out of the meeting. That never happened. It was Dean Macris, the man I worked with most of my time as a city planner. He told me supervisor White had murdered Milk and Moscone.

Michael and I joined the saddest crowd of men I'd ever seen at the intersection of Market and Castro. Quilt activist and close friend of Harvey, Cleve Jones, on a bullhorn, instructed us to walk down Market Street to City Hall peacefully. By that time, the crowd had grown beyond the intersection and masses were pouring in from the side streets. The sense of grief was a caged tiger. I was horrified at White's savagery. How could a man do that to another human being? I lost a good man in my life, and it would take time to process my sadness into something useful.?

We were given candles as we began moving out of the intersection. Bundled in the cold, I hugged men I had not seen in years, and wherever I looked, the sadness was all-consuming. As we passed the Mint, I heard a shofar being blown, and then Joan Baez was singing "Amazing Grace" in her angelic voice.

By the time I got to Civic Center, the corridor of mourners behind me stretched all the way up Market Street to Castro Street with more pouring in from side streets. That night, the queer nation mourned the death of Harvey Milk.

Dan White was sentenced to a maximum sentence of seven years and eight months in prison on May 21, 1979. I was in shock. The ruling smacked of favoritism; cops covering for cops. The inane sentence was too lenient. The sonovabitch that murdered George Moscone and Harvey Milk, the great hope of the community, got pat on the wrist! What the fuck was going on? It was bullshit!

I wasn't the Johne Ranger. Wave after wave of thousands of angry protestors bundled in jackets and parkas stormed Civic Center. Our progress towards full civil rights reached new heights when Harvey was elected, but White's judgment wiped it out by saying Harvey Milk's death was no different than a property owner being fined for failing to fix a ruptured pipe.

Next to a reflecting pond. I held Michael and we are mightier than a judge.

Speakers extolled Harvey and others voiced the communal outrage at District Attorney Joe Freitas, one time activist with Common Cause who got a law degree. Where was the justice? This was America.

A commotion rumbled behind the makeshift stage. A glass door shattered, and yelling echoed off the Beaux-Arts buildings surrounding Civic Center Plaza. An angry mob tried to find a way into City Hall. The energy continued to build

This was the first time I was this close to a mob, and it was terrifyingly scary because it had a life of its own. Once started, they couldn't be stopped, a frightening spectacular of madness. If I got within spitting distance, I'd be sucked into the madness.

The mob could explode into violence at any moment. I was quaking in my boots. *Do I go with my gut and plunge into the madness, or do I do the sensible thing and watch the mob from the safety of my home?*

The man who told me to come out had been murdered, and the best a jury of his peers could do was to tell the man who murdered him to sit in the corner. What the fuck was the jury thinking? Once again, a straight, white man, Joe Freitas, saved the ass of another straight white man.

I watched the psychology of the crowd. At first the mob had buoyancy because it didn't care what it did because they believed they had every right to be angry.

Cleve Jones's urging the crowd on raised the temperature and the crowd changed from buoyancy to revenge. They wanted blood! The pace of the night switched to fast forward and out of control. A volatile group shoved me clumsily as they raced toward the center. Then another group breached my protections, and I was caught between mobs on both sides.

I tried get out of the way and I tripped and fell. I rolled over into bushes and didn't move. When I knew it was safe, I got on a bench, and when I touched my leg, it hurt and there was blood on my hand. I took my shoe off, and the blood in my shoe spilled.

The complexion of the crowd changed again. The mob now was a vortex near the front of the podium. Like the particles of dust in the air, waves of anger radiated in ever widening circles. It was about to snatch me and hurl me into the vortex when I saw an opening and I walked as fast as I can through it to the periphery.

I hobbled up Fulton Street, and I was depleted when I slid the key into the lock. I made it as far as the living room and turned on the TV. Channel Seven had a line of cop cars ringing Civic Center Plaza engulfed in billowing smoke and angry flames. Civic Center Plaza was a full-scale war zone.

There wouldn't be another LBGTQ elected official until Roberta Achtenberg was elected to the Board of Supervisors ten years later in 1989.

Diversity

In the 1950s, San Francisco was cioppino. The first ripples on the surface were the Beatniks in the sixties who threatened the women who wore gloves at the City of Paris. The flower children who descended on the Haight Ashbury's 1967 Summer of Love broke the surface with their free love, anti-war attitudes that horrified the two parent two child families in the Sunset.

When I got to San Francisco in 1974, a line was drawn between pro-growth downtown and its vast amounts of money on one side and Calvin Welch and Sue Bierman, who'd cut their teeth stopping a freeway planned to run along the Panhandle, on the other side. Compromise was a dead, and planning commission meetings turned into blood baths that went late into the night. The fate of the city hung in the balance.

Ronald Regan was sworn in for his second term as President January 1984, and if that weren't enough to worry about,

Martin Paley, head of the San Francisco Foundation, worried the competing city interests would tear city apart.

He thought opposing sides talking to each other could ease tensions. He hired a man who drew cartoon images as he moderated contentious meetings to facilitate a retreat, and he hired me to organize the retreat.

Martin knew most of the civic leaders, so he drew up a preliminary invitation list that included Aileen Hernandez, an African American with a Spanish surname who was Long involved with civil rights, the city's Maya Angelo; Yori Wada, head of the YMCA on the boundary between the Black Western Addition and the Japanese community in Japantown and a frequent name on good citizen ballot propositions; John Jacobs, the head of the Chamber of Commerce and the San Francisco Bay Area Planning and Urban Research Association; Carl Pope, head of the Sierra Club, a prominent environmentalist, and the other leaders of the city's ethnic communities. His list had fifty names.

"Who represents the gay community?"

Martin was dumbfounded. In 1984, the head of the San Francisco Foundation that supported social service nonprofits in the city had no idea there was such a thing as the gay and lesbian community. He hadn't noticed that we had already made our own neighborhood in the previously working-class neighborhood then called Eureka Valley.

That says a lot about the upper crust's inability to acknowledge people defined by their sexuality and the closeted queer generation that didn't want to be seen. Despite Martin's deeply held convictions around fairness and his long involvement in the city's nonprofits, he didn't think he knew a queer person, and he had missed the emergence of the queer community.

The closeted generation's survival instinct to lay low reinforced the argument that if they don't know what they are looking for, they won't see us, making us invisible. But now it had detrimental effects on the community.

For us to be seen, we had to stand up for ourselves among civic leaders, so I stood up. I was seen by a group of civic leaders as the gay intelligent organizer, the first out gay person some knew.

I added Jerry Berg to his list.

I scoured available meetings places, everything from hotels to churches, and found an ideal location that would give the attendees the chance to stroll along paths that overlooked an ocean beach and was close enough to town for last minute emergencies: a resort motel in Half Moon Bay, twenty miles south of town.

I collaborated with the motel staff on their food options, making sure there were vegetarian options. I opted for the choice of salmon or pan roasted chicken as the main course. Once I knew where they would meet, I could write the invitations. Each was handwritten.

The people coming lived in various parts of the city, and each had a constituency that was constantly involving them in critical problems, so they had no reason to like each other. I had to sell them on the importance of coming together.

Nothing like this had ever been done, so Martin and I were taking a risk. The retreat could either produce familiarity among the city's diverse leaders or it could fall flat. I was nervous wreck when the moment of truth arrived. This would be the deciding moment when the retreat either succeeded or it failed. At this point, anything that either Martin or I could say would change it.

The group checked into their rooms, unpacked, and dressed for the first session. At two PM they assembled around a circle of folding tables draped with white cloth with the resort's logo in the conference room. The moderator asked them to introduce themselves, explain what they did, and describe what they expected to get from the retreat. As they went around the room, I watched body language.

I was amazed of the specialness of San Francisco that made it my home, but it was also home to them for a variety of reasons. San Francisco had an all-encompassing compassion where no one was diminished.

After witnessing the hostility of a planning commission meeting, I was dumbstruck at the change in tone. By saying something about who they were and what they expected to get from the retreat, two wanted to know what someone that they wouldn't have to answer to on the street thought about the topic under discussion.

They were equals; individuals equally concerned about a city that had a profound effect on them. They weren't the combatants battling it out

The graphic moderator, as skilled as a Disney animator, was an easy talker and he kept the group focused on his figures that summarized the group's progress as the discussion moved along. He made sure someone on both sides of an issue spoke before he moved them to the next topic.

I watched their growing comfort as they shared common concerns about a city they loved. I was impressed with their willingness to listen to each other.

When the room got overheated, I opened the large windows facing the ocean, letting a cool Pacific breeze cool them down.

The afternoon small groups of people with fixed ideas about

the subject gave them a chance to see each other in a new light. When they reported back, sharp differences emerged, and the moderator recorded them, but he never let them become arguments. By keeping track of what was said in his images, the moderator was saying, "This is the way that person feels about the subject, and I will make a note of it, so we don't forget it."

Social change starts in the mind of a single individual, and it spreads depending on how convincing that individual is and a bunch of other things. When he convinces someone of his reason for a cause, it spreads to the next person, and that repeats person to person until an entire community is convinced they need to do something. Positive change goes haywire when there are multiple arguments because an individual can only hold so many thoughts at the same time.

I don't know if any of them had ever had an intense retreat experience like the one at Half Moon Bay. I hoped a single message that diversity mattered would be the result of the retreat because if it were wishy-washy, it would be gone in a year.

I knew people leaving retreats promise to stay in touch, but once I got home, everyday life got in the way of me staying in touch with the people I'd said that to. As they left, I could only guess how what happened to them at the retreat would translate into how they treated people they disagreed with.

It was folly for me to think I could change someone's mind because only they could do it. If the retreat affected them positively, the chances are that when a crisis emerged, they would be more tolerant of the other side.

It was gratifying overhearing one of them say he learned something new.

I credit Aileen for putting word diversity into common

parlance. She understood the richness that comes from mixing races, and she knew how the cultural life of a city is enhanced when the players are on equal footing because she lived it.

Taking a job like this requires a sturdy ego because you don't get immediate satisfaction. I knew what I did, and I was content with it.

Death of a Generation

In 1981, there was a rumor of six men who shared a summer rental on Fire Island and all of them died of a mysterious illness made its way along the gay underground. I wrote it off along with the rumor that Richard Gere put a gerbil in his ass. Some conjectured it was something in the water supply on the island. More popular was the theory of a South American hustler that was spreading the deadly disease.

I took advantage of the services of San Francisco's free, anonymous VD clinic several times.so if six gay men died, I knew whatever it was had to be a new strain of a venereal disease, and I wanted it to stay on the East Coast. Gay men were having a lot of sex, so it was inevitable that we would have cases on the West Coast. It was just a matter of time.

Dick Gamble was a large man and incredibly good looking. He worked at the Planning Department when I worked there before transferring to the Mayor's Office in City Hall. At first because good looking men were straight, I was certain Dick was straight. That changed when he invited me to a barbeque on property he owned in Sonoma County. My only other exposure to a group of gay men at a party was in graduate school in Philadelphia. In the middle of a Sunday afternoon soiree in student's home, everyone raced upstairs. By the time I got there panting, they were at a window pointing and giggling. Below them and across the street in the backyard of a row house on Naudain Street a gaggle of men in caftans and clogs was having brunch. I recoiled at the caftans and clogs because there was nothing masculine about them.

I wasn't out, and I discovered shortly after getting to Dick's barbeque that I knew the men were queens. Five or ten years older, big men. They were successful professionals. One of them tried to put the make on me. A large man that I don't know who being expected me to want to have sex with him gave me the creeps.

It was only after I was back in the city that I heard rumors of Dick's parties notorious for the vast amount of marzipan and debauchery.

Long before AIDS, Dick was in the hospital. The disease had shrunk his build and his eyes looked tired. He said his doctor told him that something had infected his blood. To cheer him up, I told him the Czar of Russia had hemophilia, so he was in good company. That was a painful metaphor. It was the last time I saw Dick. He died from AIDS.

Tommy Doyle was my first fist bud. I liked him because I could count on him; he was always ready to play. He could be ready in thirty minutes. It took me an hour. Living on 18th Street meant his home was convenient for quickies on my lunch breaks. When I stopped by one day in 1982, he had just come back from a trip to Mexico. He said because he'd been tired, so he went there to rest. He planned to go to the beach every day, but when he climbed the hill back to his car the second day, he was out of breath. He didn't get better and spent the rest of the week in bed.

Two weeks after that, I was asked to be part of his care team. I brought him dinner every Thursday. Tommy was a musician, and he was member of the Gay Men's Chorus. He never got better, but for a while, he didn't get worse, so I never knew if he was going to live or die. That was before AIDS was known to be a one-way ticket, so no one knew what his symptoms meant.

On one visit he let me play his brand-new Yamaha piano that let him record what he played. It could also play music. He tolerated my "Somewhere Over the Rainbow," but I could tell he was tired.

I had a trip to Hawaii planned months in advance, and when I came back, Tommy had died. I put Tommy's name on the plaque on the outside of the Hormel LGBTQI Center at the library because he would have been part of the campaign. I also put vocalist Sylvester's name on the plaque because he deserved to be there.

Not knowing what caused men to die was a corridor of endless doors. One of the doors would have the answer but it stretched into the distance. Every door I tried opened was an empty room. One didn't have a floor. I got to what I thought was the end, but when I turned, and the corridor ahead of me was as long as the one I'd just come down, but I knew the answer to this mysterious illness was out there somewhere.

I needed any bit of information, and the lack of it infuriated me. I felt helpless. American science touted itself as the best in the world, so they should have identified the disease a month after the first outbreak. That was two years ago.

When the fuck are our great scientist going to find the virus, bacteria or fungus that's killing gay men? The deaths must stop.

Each week, instead of good news, photos on the Obituary page of the *Bay Area Reporter* went from one to three. A month later there were seven.

Stories of miracle cures kept popping up all over the place. Some were as simple as a change in a man's diet. Another was a drug in Japan that was illegal in the States. I heard of a man who flew empty suitcases to Japan, filled them with the drug, and smuggled them back to the States.

Each miracle cure got me excited; this was the end of death! After years of not knowing anything, I was relieved there was an end in sight. A month later, the cure didn't work, and that compounded my despair.

One of the hottest crazes was Louise Hay. She authored a book *You Can Heal Your Life*. Her self-help attitude captured the imagination of men who needed answers and needed them fast. Men chartered two planes to fly them from San Francisco to LA to hear her speak. I spoke with one of the men who was about to fly. He was convinced that she could cure him, and his argument was compelling; our mental state does influence what goes on in our body made sense. I'm wary of get rich quick schemes, so I never bought her book,

When I heard that a friend who'd flown to LA to hear Louise died, I wasn't sure there would ever be an end to AIDS.

It angered me that our Kaiser doc, who knew Michael had a bout with Hep C, didn't give him a drug that boosted his white blood cells. He was desperate to find a cure that would keep him alive, and once he believed wheat grass was going to save him, he grew it on the back porch. He made smoothies with it. It stained the sink green. He believed in it until the day he died.

He didn't trust modern medicine because modern medicine didn't keep his mother from dying of breast cancer. Michael Petrelis, an AIDS activist, accused the makers of AZT of lining their pockets and he questioned the effectiveness of AZT.

Michael read Petrelis' argument as a reason not to take AZT, so he refused to take it when it was first available. I was desperate because he was the most important force in my life, so I urged him to drink Ensure. He wasn't getting better, and eventually I had to talk him into taking AZT. Because he didn't want it, his body wasn't receptive to it. By that time, his bout of Hep C had weakened his immune system, the chemo treatments weakened it further, and mycobacterium avium complex MAC. was eroding his digestive system.

In retrospect, it was his disease, and he should have been the final arbiter of what was going to save him.

The federal government's response to the crisis was pathetic and homophobic. Jesse Helms, senator from North Carolina, called for gay men to be quarantined. Once the disease had a name, President Ronald Reagan refused to say the word *AIDS*. His administration kept scientists from saying how sad things were.

It also hoped the disease would go away. We were chomping at the bit for them to get their ass in gear. Men I knew from the bars were fun loving, gentle souls, but when their lives were on the line, they became fierce warriors. The first wave of ACT UP and other Northern California activists insisted scientists find the source of the disease. Until we knew what was killing gay man, they couldn't start work on a treatment. They had to know the agent.

Once HIV was identified, activists staged demonstrations at the offices of the Federal Drug Administration and a major pharmaceutical company demanding they speed up the approval process of new drugs. We needed action, our friends and lovers were dying.

French scientist Luc Montagnier of the Pasteur Institute in Paris discovered the virus in 1983. Now that we knew what it was, I wanted action on it, but American scientist Robert Gallo wanted credit for his work.

The Reagan administration didn't want to look like it had its head up its ass, and it took months for them to work out an agreement with Montagnier. Meanwhile, men were dying in greater numbers.

A disease that killed gay men was low hanging fruit for Republicans. To assure their base of their faith in God, they scapegoated gay men's sexual freedom as the cause of our deaths. We deserved to die.

We were a new community, but AIDS galvanized us into a fighting force. We had to change the minds of Americans, many who thought being gay was a choice. Hemophiliacs were dying from AIDS and so were people from Haiti. The American public not only had to recognize that we were decent human beings, but they also had to understand that AIDS wasn't just affecting gay men. AIDS wasn't a gay crisis; it was a health crisis.

Now, instead of actively seeking to assure basic civil rights for the community, activist Bill Kraus, who worked for Congressman Phil Burton, became involved with AIDS, and he was an active proponent for closing the baths.

Obituaries now took up two pages.

This was a terrible time for the community because we

were badly split on the best way to deal with AIDS. Roommates stopped talking to each other.

The turning point came in 1985 when Rock Hudson announced he had AIDS. Just as he tried to keep his sexuality a secret, he was reluctant to be public about AIDS. Armistead Maupin was one of the people who convinced him to come out. Rock's greatest legacy is not the films he made with Doris Day that made him America's sweetheart, but his courage to come out about AIDS. That decision had more to do with changing American's attitudes than anything else.

Just like the politicians when I started with HRCF who refused gay money, these politicians didn't want to be associated with a "gay disease." Only a few members of Congress like Henry Waxman of California worked on behalf of AIDS. Members of prominent families got sick and died. With the affluent dealing with AIDS, politicians who took their money had to deal with AIDS.

The federal government wouldn't fund AIDS assistance until July 1983.

Before AIDS had a name, my first memorial service was a service for a man named Peter. He disowned his family and went only by the name Peter. You don't disown your family when an inheritance is at stake, but he might have been on to something.

The service was held in a hall in the Mission. The darkened room had lines of folding chairs along a center aisle. The altar was an oak table covered with a gold edged, white linen sheet. One side had a large vase of white peonies, the other was empty.

Peter loved music. The program for the service listed two

speakers and six musical performances. The performance that sticks in my mind is a soprano and a mezzo-soprano singing a duet from Bellini's *Norma*. When their voices soared, it sent shivers down my spine.

I marveled that Peter's friends had gone to such lengths for his memorial service because we never did that in Wausau. I was still new to the city, and I had a lot to learn.

My second memorial service was for a young man everyone loved. Doug Franks was cute as a button, and you just had to love him. Doug came from a working-class family but graduated from the College of Marin. The Swedenborgian Church looked right out of the Shire in Middle-earth, and it was the perfect setting to remember the adorable little guy. When the organ began, my tears flowed. Another beautiful soul was lost.

I'm not a crier. With John's abuse growing up, I cried every day until my twelfth birthday. After that, I kept myself from crying and I stowed my sadness and hurts in an old ammo case.

The third was a traditional funeral service in Saint Ignatius Catholic Church. Catholics tell me rituals are important, and there are a lot of them. The rituals meant nothing to me, so the long service bored me. I tried to hide my boredom because it was a funeral service. The officiating priest knew David Smith Fox and his family, so his homily was personal. There were so many people in the church it felt like a mass event that could have happened anywhere.

That saddened me because I wanted gay men to be changemakers until the day they died.

When the 21st century began, almost nine thousand people mostly gay men in San Franisco had died of AIDS.

Be a Leader

Being a leader was tricky because I didn't fit the classic leader mold, someone driven by a cause, eloquent speaker, and inspires thousands of followers. That's not me. Once I start a project, doing the best I'm capable of, I want to complete it as thoroughly as possible. I don't like wasting time because there's always something on the horizon that needs attention.

My self-confidence got beaten out of me at the dinner table, the only time the family was in the same room. When I had an original idea about doing something we always did differently, older brother John put me down. Dad had to be right about everything he said. I matured earlier than most boys my age, and I developed a fine sensitivity to understanding what people mean when they say something because it's not always the same thing as what they say. An example, Dad said, "We go to Alice's on Sunday because her sunroom is the best place to watch Sunday football." I said, "You like her more than Mom." He replied, "That is not what I said." I left it there because I expected he would pay for college and graduate school, and I'd inherit something when he died, and I had to survive Long enough to reach the promised land.

At the time, I wouldn't have guessed the promised land was San Francisco because I thought the culture and art I sought I'd only find on the East Coast, and San Franciso then was just a city of freaks thousands of miles away, and the *Rice-A-Roni, the San Francisco Treat* ad on TV.

I took my frustration out on myself, convinced I was inadequate.

I wasn't a popular kid in high school, but kids running for student council president or homecoming queen, insisted I run their campaign because I was the only kid smart enough to do it. That set me apart, so I downplayed being a leader.

I recently went on Amazon and looked for leadership books, and there were enough to choke a horse. I did a leadership training program, and it didn't take me much time to realize true leadership can't be taught. A person is a leader, or they aren't. Leadership is a trait; it's not something you can teach someone. The corollary is a follower. Being a good follower is an art, and a good follower is just as crucial to the success of a project. My work depended on them.

Paul Niebanck saw my instincts for leadership. He taught me how to think. Being the smartest guy in class, I was used to think I had all the answers, but Paul disabused me of that by insisting I see a problem from multiple points of view and to try to see why the people who had the opposite opinion from mine had that opinion. I should understand why they feel the way they do.

He taught me problem-solving is a journey that starts by recognizing how much I don't know about the problem and the resources at my disposal.

Coming up with a quick solution is easy, but Paul had me examine the implications of various alternative decisions and how one decision affects a everything else before I started thinking of a conclusion. That ran counter to my impatience, and even my quick thinking wasn't good enough for Paul. He wanted me to be exhaustive. I should understand both the good and the adverse consequences of a decision before I begin addressing it.

Jerry Berg also saw my leadership potential and over the years, he connected me with people he thought I should know. Jerry was eight years older with more experience with local politics. He was full of himself, but his size and his determination made him a formidable character. Much of the social infrastructure in the community in San Francisco is the result of his work because he did the legal work every nonprofit needs to get its 501(c)3 status. Without it they can't raise money.

I benefitted from his powers to make things happen the day that Michael and I, with Jerry and his partner, Jim Proby, got to a Linda Ronstadt concert at the Greek Theater late. It was crowded as hell, but when Jerry stood at the end of row of benches, four people got up to make room for us. Could have been a coincidence, but I like to think he made it happen, just like he made things happen when I needed them when I did the first HRCF dinner.

He invited me to be join a men's group that included the community's best thinkers and men who started community organizations like Tom Waddell, the Olympic medalist who founded the Gay Olympics and philanthropist Jim Hormel. I belonged to the group twelve years and many now dead I consider brothers. They were invited to any party I hosted, and the library campaign would not have succeeded if it weren't for them.

They were more like me than the men I was fisting, although one man overlapped. B. was a gentleman of the South of the highest caliber. He told me the story of him being at an early men's retreat. The hippie leading the retreat asked everyone to describe the most meaningful event in his life. They went around the room, and when it was B.'s turn, he said the most meaningful event in his life was the time his boyfriend had his hand in his ass as he read him the *Desideratum*. How cool is that?

Jerry introduced me to the power of being present, and he prided himself on being a self-made person, but he went overboard with Werner Erhart's Erhard Seminars Training's in-depth personal and professional training; Est was his compass and bible. It got him into real trouble at the beginning of the AIDS epidemic.

He believed his EST training, homeopathic medicine and phone consultations with an expensive big-name guru would keep him from being infected. He never got tested. Sadly, Jerry was human.

He and Jim moved to outside Santa Fe, New Mexico, because he believed the area was crisscrossed by powerful healing energies. I visited him there, and I was crushed when I saw him in a make-shift hospital bed weak and helpless.

What was even sadder was that after him drilling into me the importance of taking responsibility for my thoughts and actions, that I took to heart, he abused Jim ruthlessly. He treated him like his slave, and he could do nothing right. Jerry was never satisfied with anything that Jim did around the house.

Jerry needed professional care, and I wanted to intervene, but I'm not a therapist.

He died a couple of weeks after I left. After Jerry died, Michael went to Santa Fe to be with Jim. Jim died months later.

Jerry Berg wasn't perfect, but I remember him as the tall, handsome full of himself visionary who taught me what it means to be responsible leader.

Sex

"A nymphomaniac is someone who has more sex than you do."
–Dr. Alfred Kinsey

Erotica

Sex has always fascinated me and let me say upfront, my interest was selfish. I had sex because I needed to be needed. Before I was five, I did the "I'll show me mine if you showed me yours" thing with two girls, and I was fascinated about the way their vaginas slipped under them. I was expecting more. I asked David Schilling to peel back the foreskin I'd never seen and expose the head of his dick when we were in a bathtub. I watched Ronny Yonke take a shit on the bustled floorboards in Ms. Coates' shed. I was curious, and I wanted to see how the machinery operated. In Scout camp boys bragged about making white stuff, but I didn't know what they were talking about, and I wrote it off to something only adults know. One night at Scout Camp, a redhead a couple of years older from a troop in Rhinelander selected me as the only boy in the cabin to expose his erection inside his sleeping bag. I wanted to touch it. I don't remember my first erection, but I remember cuddling with Perry at Scout Camp. Being that close to him felt so good. I couldn't get enough of it, and he was patient with me.

I gotta be honest and say that seeing Dad's dick in the shower did not turn me on. He was emotionally cold, so there were never any vibes from him. Despite it being a large home, the shower was a one-man shower at best, so my glimpse was brief, but rather than turning me on, it confirmed he had a dick. The first thing that got me hard was seeing the outline of an erection in a boy's white cotton briefs. That was my Mt. Everest. When I made a boy hard, I got hard, and I knew I wasn't crazy.

My first interest was cock. As a teenager in the fifties, every dick in town was hiding behind layers of clothing. If it were left outside, it would freeze solid as ice. Ever resourceful, I signed-on as assistant to the football and basketball coaches which meant I handed out towels to the teams as they entered a gang shower where their junk was on full display. The classes before mine could easily have taken a towel from the stack of rolled white towels, but the class of 1961 and the class of 1962 had their towels handed to them. My world changed when the Universe provided a copy of *Physique Pictoral*, and I fixed on the posing straps.

When Clay fucked me the first time, my interest switched to ass, and once I got into fisting, I got hard when I felt his ass grip my hand. I don't know if that makes me a top or a bottom, I use versatile that best described me.

Verbal and visual erotica taught me a lot about sex. John Rechy's *City of Night* was the first time I saw a gay man in print, and seeing him in print made him real. When the Lambda Literary Foundation was just one staff person and a smattering of volunteers ready for any content, I was the erotica editor. I apologize to the authors of the books I reviewed because when

I wrote them, I knew jackshit about writing criticism, and they deserve better.

There's hardcore written erotica with throbbing manmeat and dripping pussies, and intelligent erotica that leaves much to the imagination. There is some of the latter here.

Boyd McDonald wrote a series of chapbooks with stories of farmboys having their first sex in a barn and a horny boy giving blowjobs to truckers in the men's room of a gas station at the edge of town in graphic detail that were published in a magazine entitled *Straight to Hell* or *The Manhattan Review of Unnatural Acts*. Their rawness fueled my early jack off fantasies, and they also did it for me when I first came out because they were familiar. McDonald claimed they were originals, but I've read enough to see he put his touch on some of them.

They are gay cult classics, and I am donating my extensive collection of his work to the Gay and Lesbian Historical Society.

Visual erotica that turned me on were the spreads of hot men in dirty magazines, and there is an example of that.

When I was fourteen, *Physique Pictorial* was my bible. It was a small chapbook with pictures and drawings of a naked man leaning on a Corinthian capital shot from the side, so you didn't see his dick. Other men were draped over each other as a tableau, and there were drawings of locker rooms of naked me with no dick showing, their excuse for art to get them past the censors.

What got me hard fire fast were the posing straps, just enough fabric to mold around his dick and balls. The hottest were the straps where if I looked very closely, I could imagine the faint outline of his dick. In Wausau in the fifties, dicks were invisible, so I made do with posing straps. A great deal of teenage jism was expressed with a posing strap throbbing my brain.

The first dirty movie I saw in the dark room of a neighbor's home was a reel-to-reel that kept breaking of nude middle-aged men playing volleyball, the best pornographers could get away with in the forties. It embarrassed me.

The gay community has a stable of fine porn filmmakers like Wakefield Poole. When I came out, video arcades with booths big enough for a man to stand were all over the place. The booths had a machine, and for a quarter, I could watch eight minutes of young men having sex. They were amateurish and not particularly erotic.

On a Christmas visit in the eighties, I discovered Wausau's porno arcade. As I wandered the darkness, I saw a younger, contemporary of Robert's, the last person in the world I'd have sex with. At least the gay men in Wausau had an outlet.

Chuck Holmes ran Falcon Studios, the premier purveyor of gay porn. I was in his office, and because his talent was among the best in the business, I expected he had scouts, like baseball teams have scouts, that toured North America and Europe with an eye for hot prospects. I asked him where he found his talent, and he said they came to him.

Imagine a sweet looking, scrawny kid in a small town in Tennessee who was bullied by a jock at school sees a dirty magazine his older brother stashed under dirty clothes in the closet. He thinks he has what it takes to be a porn actor. He works out at home using weights, and his body starts looking muscular. He looks in the mirror several times until he decides he is ready for prime time. He packs a duffle bag with a change of clothes, clean underwear, and a picture of the porn star he uses for inspiration, and he takes a Greyhound to San Francisco and presents himself at Chuck's door. A porn star is born.

Paul Merar was a darkhaired, large man with dashing

European style and a superb set of muscles. He was a Sierra Club librarian and my entre into the porno industry. I met him through Clay. He was a skilled player, and he told me I had more sex than anyone he knew. I took that as a compliment. He was in a couple of minor porno movies I never saw. He was also a sex worker, and he said most of the men he went home with just wanted companionship.

Stupid me, I thought sex workers all had sex. Gay men can lead Lonely lives, so it makes sense that a gay man would buy human company. That works out for both of them because one makes money being cordial, and the other has someone to hold and listen to him for a certain amount of time.

Two porno videos were shot in my flat on Fulton Street, and that's when I got acquainted with a lot of the down time and people just sitting around that's involved in making a porn film. It's not sexy. There's equipment and staff all over the place.

I call one of the videos "The Cancelled Check." The production company imported a good-looking hunk from the Czech Republic. He looked the part; tall, board shoulders, powerful head, meaty dick. On Saturday, they shot what the director described as the warmup scene. Naked men in my shower room shaving, making eye contact, sucking dick under streams of hot water. Shots of naked feet on the shower room floor.

Sunday was the cum shot, but they can't find him. When it's been over an hour since he was supposed to be there, they send out a search party. An hour later, they find him, and he's wasted. He was up until 6 AM on speed fucking his brains out. He wanted my Viagra and one of my dirty magazines. I can still see him bent over the magazine on top of a large mahogany case once a record player, trying to get hard. They shot the scene, but they never used it because his lackluster performance dragged the video's hotness.

When I was doing the library campaign, Durk Dehner, president of the Tom of Finland Foundation, asked me if the Gay and Lesbian Center would take the Tom of Finland estate's works of Tom's. I wanted the collection of the cultural icon bad, but the library didn't have staff that curated art. The more I know about curating, the more I'm blown away by precision of the craft, so I regrettably understand why the library couldn't accept the work. I contacted a closeted gay man who had a powerful (think lots of money) position on the board of the San Francisco Museum of Modern Art to see if the museum would take the collection. He said he would check with the board chair, and the board chair danced away from it faster than the Roadrunner.

He made a grievous artistic judgment, and I bet he's kicking himself now for not taking the Tom of Finland collection

Erotica is the way some gay men learn how to be gay, so it's a vital part of our history. It may soon come under fire from the conservatives on the Supreme Court.

Buddy's Amazing Adventure
a faerie tale

Once upon a time in faraway Landsdorf, Buddy Benson hears his grandfather is dying. Buddy holds fast to that last time he saw him as the sun rainbowed the snow-white hair flowing over his shoulders.

On the outgoing tide aboard the fastest ship in the fleet, Captain Barnstable who always returns to port with holds of the finest spices assures Buddy that he'll make his destination on time. Comforted, Buddy slips into a cozy berth and falls fast asleep. As the ship rocks on even tides, he dreams his grandfather rises from his bed and takes him back to Greater Promethea where the sun shines every day.

On the darkest night of the year a once in a century storm trounces the sea. The sky blacks out and sixty-foot waves toss the ship like Buddy's toy boat in the tub. At the height of the storm, a mean-spirited wave hurls Buddy from his berth, and later a kinder wave flushes him out of a hatch. He drifts atop a steamer trunk with sweat his only sustenance.

Entangled in waterlogged canvas delirious he washes up on a porous shore. He is barely conscious when the sun turns the horizon bloody crimson, and a deep masculine voice breaks the silence. "You're early."

"What?" Buddy spits the sand in his teeth.

"You aren't far enough along." The resonant tone reveals nothing.

"Grandfather's dying." He starts to cry, and a bearded face emerges through his tears.

"You're here before your time."

"Who are you?"

"Let's get you cleaned up."

Guided by Bearded Man, Buddy makes his way barefoot through menacing shrubberies. Fifty paces past a stream of luminous fish Buddy comes upon handsome men entwined in each other on a bed of moss. He checks with Bearded Man to see what he should do, and Bearded Man vanishes in a spritz of mist. Pulling moss from golden locks one of the men signals, but Buddy likes the eyes of the dark-haired man who's avoiding him. "I don't want to intrude," Bearded Man appears in a whirl of mist and after his agreeing nod, Buddy moves on.

Further on, high above a field of grazing Long-haired sheep, a Jumbotron runs a loop announcing the death of his grandfather. The repetition drives broken Buddy bonkers, and he soaks himself in tears. His grandfather insisted he never give up, so later in the day, Buddy struggles on.

A space has been carved from solid red granite and cracks at just the right place make it a gang shower of thermal-heated water. Beneath one of the showers a muscular Asian man and a lithe white man lathed each but as their hands glide over the other's body there are no tiny iridescent bubbles no sign of soap. Under another shower, a man in a tuxedo jacket plays checkers with a naked Black man with a braided ponytail.

When they see Buddy, they shift into camp, and with hands on hips, they pantomime dropping the soap in wild outsized gestures. They are having so much fun the men under the other shower join them buffooning. Hearing their raucous laughter, men emerge from within the cave with platters of succulent savories over their heads. A fine mahogany table appears in a cloud of fog, and the platters float out of their hands and float to their place at the table. The men now kerchiefed in snow-white napkins, gather around the delicacies in brotherly camaraderie, and with much groping and feeding grease-streaked cheeks, a feast commences.

Toweled off and smelling of sugar Buddy is ready to take on the day. He turns to leave and the path to the cave is now a neighborhood street with outdoor seating under Technicolor umbrellas, a gay bar, and Cliff's Hardware. Buddy's eyes are big as saucers as he imagines himself in the heavily sequined jockstrap in Cliff's Halloween window. In a blitz of mist, Bearded Man appears behind him and gently takes him to the back of the store. Befuddled Buddy bunches against Betty Boop bathmats. Bearded Man presses a rack of Venetian Mardi gras masks, and the rack of masks opens to a book-lined library, Oriental carpets, two chairs, and a desk.

"Have a seat." Bearded Man swings a wing chair around for Buddy and sits behind a warmly polished partner's desk that smells of sugar and red wine vinegar.

Once Buddy has seated a little person in a top hat slips out of a disguised as a bookcase door and hands Bearded Man a kidskin folder. Bearded Man runs his finger down the list in the folder. "You surprised us." Pleased, the little person turns and disappears behind the disguised as a bookcase door.

"Please tell me what's happening." Buddy is close to losing it.

"You passed with flying colors."

"You killed Gramps, fucker." With fists clenched Biddy goes for Bearded Man but an invisible force stops him.

"Do not make for yourself a carved image." His resonant tone reveals nothing.

"That's from the Bible." Buddy looks around to see if anyone from his church can see him.

"Your grandfather was flawed. He murdered when stationed in Nam."

"Is that why you brought me here, to punish me?"

"You are here to be tested. Our Creator in the Great Bathhouse in Sky made the Isle of Men a paradise so gifted men like you can fulfill your sexual potential. That freedom does not come cheap. On the Isle, one must first prove he's responsible. When you saw that your grandfather died you didn't blame the doctors for not keeping him alive. When you were asked to join the couple having sex, you knew their love was pure and you left them alone. You were as hard as the granite of the cave, but you did not intrude on the others' fun. On the Isle, we call that having your shit together, and we only permit men who have their shit together to remain on the Isle."

With Bearded Man's spirit swirling throughout him, Buddy becomes a man, and he marvels at his transformation as a man.

Bearded Man opens the curtain behind him open to an array of two men leaving a three-story Victorian with a sign over the door that reads Playhouse and men of varying sizes making out on a perfect white sand beach. He detects motion in the bushes behind the beach,

"When do I get started?" Buddy flutters like a butterfly.

"The way we do things here is you start by making friends and because the bond made between you must last your lifetimes, you make friends by having sex with them first. There are three stages with various levels of sexual involvement at each, and if we've chosen correctly our learners will make it to all three, and so far, that has proven true.

"I want it all."

"Ah youth. In time, you like our other novices will understand why we put such an emphasis on pacing. Sexual freedom is a powerful drug, and since we have the finest here, we don't want our learners burning out."

"Sign me up." His eyes bright with excitement.

"In your first year, you must engage in oral and anal sex with at least five hundred men. Some of our quickest learners pushed through in less than a year, and they went on to more experimental sex."

"Oh yeah! Sure."

"I know what you're thinking. They did not do that on speed or ecstasy. That men need speed to open their holes is one of the great fallacies of the old days. Our studies show that all amphetamines do permanent damage to the brain. We want our players clean of harmful drugs, so they are able to fulfill their dreams of sexual excellence."

"Really?"

"Free marijuana, psilocybin mushrooms, and LSD are available throughout the Isle because our tests prove they are the most effective means of expanding minds as well as fueling imaginations, the perfect recipe of mind-blowing sex.

"What about the shit?" His face beet red.

"I hear that a lot, but we don't condemn, rather before they play our players must be well versed in everything available to them in our vast library of sex. I'm immensely proud of our collection, and I'm particularly excited about a new cache of ancient texts from sexual masters in Sumatra. We tried to get them for years, but we kept having trouble with Customs. We have a division devoted to finding the best and most explicit literature about male sex, and we finally have a curator for that collection who comes to us from his years as Director of the Stier Menschliche Sexualität Instit in Berlin."

"The what?" Buddy asks impatiently.

"Pardon me I got distracted. No man on the Isle has anal sex with shit in his hole. You didn't see it because of the mist, but just past the first bend in the cave, we have a room dedicated to cleansing holes. There are places to lounge as well as douche hoses and buckets kept fresh with bleach to clean the nozzles because we want the experience to be pleasurable. Hygiene is paramount on the Isle."

"You don't mess around."

"Most of the men who are here to develop their anal skills go on to develop fisting skills, and because as you will soon learn if you don't already know, your hole produces the most joy per square inch of any body part. We have afternoon sessions devoted entirely to expanding the range of holes."

"Yeah, I know about holes. Criminy! I'm twenty-two."

"When you're at the second level. combining fisting and yoga has made both easier for some of our learners to master. When you get to the second level, some model themselves after swamis in India that after years of training can inhale thick hemp rope deep into their holes, but instead of hemp rope that

is rough even with gobs of lube, they are creative in what they inhale into their holes."

"You gotta be kidding me." Conflicting messages ricochet like rubber bullets.

"Take a deep breath. I know this is a lot to absorb in such a brief period of time. He waits.

There you go. Nice and easy. ..... Ready for more?

"Ready."

"I should have mentioned earlier that all styles of sex top and bottom are equally important because we want our men to take full advantage of what the Isle has to offer and experience the full range of human sexual expression."

"That's it? I want more." There is rustling in his loins.

"Enough shoptalk. I haven't explained Star Level that's been a mighty challenge for our advanced learners, and we're so proud of the men that make Star. Our Creator picked a winner in you, and I'm confident that you'll go about composing your repertoire the way I composed mine by playing with men at your level or higher,"

"Tell me about Star!!!" He shakes his fists.

"Patience my son. You will learn about that when you are second level.

"Are you telling me in the meantime I have to have sex with all the men on the Isle?"

"What fool wouldn't you want to have sex with them?"

The plaque secured to a prominent wall in the Streetcar Named Desire dining hall with much cheering reads:

Brother Buddy spent many rewarding years at Star level with tar and Leopard both Star Level when he washed up. Perfectionist that he was, with his finely tuned techniques, Buddy treated the men on the Isle to the finest hours of their lives. His death at one hundred and ten of natural causes was mourned by the thousands of men he had sex with and those who modeled their lives after his. Buddy was a gentleman of the highest order, and he remains forever in our hearts.

Poem

Sex starts the second I'm touched.
    Once I know where his head is at
        It's raw instinct.
            My instinctive response
                is honest
                    It gets messy

Do not forget the seams, the corners
    Where the body parts are joined,
        the narrow strip between
            the belly and the thigh.
                It's a raceway.

Chance Encounter

I was on my lunch break from City Hall in 1979. I made it as far down Castro Street as the Italian deli, where hard sausages dangled enticements from cast iron rods and soft cheeses begged me to slip a thick wedge onto my tongue. The sidewalk had a fine layer of residue of fairie dust from last night's revelries and approaching from the south was Drew Okun "Al Parker" in all his splendid masculinity and his manager, a dark-haired man who looked like he was having a bad day.

I'd had major hots for Al Parker ever since seeing a spread of him in a skin magazine in the dirty bookstore on 18th Street. He emanated sex, and it was hard to turn the page. I'd already gone back several times for the explicit purpose of looking at him, and each time my dick swelled as it swelled the last time.

I don't get a chance like this every day, so as I passed Drew, I look him in the eye. Thinking he would have no interest in me, I swiveled curious to see how he responded. He was looking back. I didn't stop to think this was happening because instincts kicked in. I caught up with him extending my hand. "Would you like to come back to our place?" Drew's guy-next-door smile lit the street.

After a nod from his grumpy manager, Drew said, "Sure."

I was so excited I peed my pants as I scribbled my address and phone number on a bar napkin. After a quick, "See you in a bit," I raced breathlessly to Toad Hall and dragged Michael out from behind the bar. "You won't believe what just happened."

"What?"

"We have a date with a porn star."

Minutes later, nonplussed Michael and I, squirming like a fish out of water, sped along Divisadero Street. I never had sex with a porn star, but I was about to have sex with the porn star of porn stars. Was this really happening? I couldn't believe my good luck. As I parked in the garage, I whispered, "Thank you, Universe."

Upstairs, my mind was going a mile a minute as I prepped the bed for play. I cleaned out in the shower. As I hastily collected the grease, paper towels, and poppers racing around the flat, I vacillated between knowing that sex with Al Parker was going to be amazing and knowing that waiting for a doorbell that never rings was folly.

My years of training by some of the best players were about to be tested, and it was imperative that I be on my A-game because I was pitting skills against a man who was one of the most successful at having sex with men in front of a camera. I could not screw it up. That put me in play mode, and it sidelined my agitated nerves.

The doorbell rang, and I flew down three flights of stairs

ready as I would ever be to show Al Parker how hard I'd worked hard at getting this good at sex.

At the top of the stairs, out of breath, I took his coat and hung it in the closet. When I turned, I was standing face to face with Drew Okum. Not Al Parker, the sensuous selection of sinew, but Drew Okum, a man like me. He appreciated being asked to have sex by a man of similar sexual energy. It was a straightforward request to join him having sex.

Drew's dick looked just as good in person as it did in the magazine. Touching his nicely muscled body was far better than seeing it in videos or on paper. I liked his energy. He was just as interested in showing my ass a fabulous time as I was interested in doing the same to him. He had no qualms about being a bottom. I lay back and watched as Michael showed him what he could do, the slurping sound music to my ears.

Sex was the major reason he got into porno. He wasn't the college football star quarter back with a huge schlong that was awkward at sex. Drew considered sex a calling, and he worked at being good at it. I respected that, and when he was asked by me who considered sex a sport, he was being asked to have sex with an equal, which didn't happen all the time, he said. I broke through the protection he needed as a celebrity.

He knew Al Parker was a rock star but was warm and casual, and he carried his perfectly proportioned body with no shame. My kind of playmate.

The three of us knew why we are there, so we undressed, and sizing each other up we climb onto the sleigh bed that Michael and I slept in. By the time our lips met, his mere presence was already teasing me and getting me hard. Tongues slipped in and out as the three of us entwined. I watched to make sure that Michael was being treated equally, and Drew was an equal opportunity player.

I will let you imagine having sex with Al Parker because that will be more vivid for you than my words.

Close your eyes. What does he feel like?

What was it like for you?

With sun casting ladders, I was on my A game and having the best time of my life. His fully dressed manager sat idly by; he'd no doubt seen it all.

After hours of strenuous, sweaty sex with Michael just as engaged as me, the three of us were pools of perfect pleasure. I just had sex with the man I was madly in love with and a porn star that I'd had the hots for. It doesn't get better than that.

Drew had a paying customer appointment, so he grabbed a quick shower. He stepped out with a towel around his waist and said he thought the *trompe l'oeil* was real when he first saw it.

I pinched my wrist to remind me I just had fire in the hole sex with Al Parker. Times like that are only supposed to occur in Falcon Studio VCR tapes, but it was happening in real time in the home I shared with Michael. For those who don't know, VCR tapes were an early version of DVD.

At the top of the stairs, we bear-hugged with bodies still warm from sex. Before descending, he whispered, "Good job."

With Drew in our bedroom, the setting was ripe for me hogging Al Parker, and Michael feeling rejected. He and I learned how to stay connected when we played with others, so our time with Drew didn't erupt in Michael storming out of the room.

If you'd been there, you would have seen a continuous flow of sensuous male connection.

Michael and I were that good.

Forty Years Handball

Throughout history, the men who fist relied on the kindness of strangers. The Catacombs, the Hothouse, the Sling, and Hickory Street chart the trajectory of my career as a handballer.

The Catacombs was my maiden voyage, but scholarship on the era was scant. From what I gathered from men who knew the Catacombs, it started as a play party in Steve McEachern's living room. The party must have gone well for all concerned because over time, interest in fisting grew. It reached a tipping point, and they couldn't accommodate everyone in their living room. The basement of their Victorian on 21st Street in the Mission was a large space. With a fresh coat of paint on the walls and scrubbing the grit off the concrete floors, Steve and his partner of many years had a play space large enough for their extended group. Steve told me, "Once it got started, someone called it the Catacombs."

Every Thursday at seven PM I got the call, "Hi, this is Steve. Will I see you Saturday?" The first space of the Catacombs had a Long wooden bar that curved down one side of the room. The opposite wall had tall thick wooden benches with space underneath to store clothing. I squeezed around the black waterbed I never used that occupied most of the middle room with just enough space a dog-sized alcove; it was painted black. The third and largest room at the back was painted gray, and it was a few steps down, so I could stand at the top of the steps and get a feel for the night before getting down into the action on the floor. A sheet of Masonite on a wall held dildos silhouetted in black, so when I was out of my mind on dope, I knew where to put the dumb thing when I was finished using it. There were medium-grade rubber mats on the floor for fucking and two slings with a communal giant drum of Crisco suspended between them. This was before AIDS and safe sex, so men playing in both slings used the same Crisco throughout the night. One night, Jerry Green stood out because he was the only man there that was really into having fun. He had a finely muscled body and Italian sensuality. I was played in a corner when he fucked me crazy. I played with him a second time in New York where I fisted him on top of the Mind Shaft on cool night watching the lights of the buildings on the other side of the Hudson River. At that time, he ran the kitchen at the Guggenheim Museum. He moved to LA and opened a café on Santa Monica Blvd. I visited him at his home in LA. He said he was tired and expected after a day of rest he could get back to his dream. I didn't hear from him for some time, and a friend called to say he died. Then I saw a story about a Jerry Green who opened a restaurant on Santa Monica Blvd, so I knew it was the same man who infected me with HIV.

Now, I have no idea when I go infected or by whom because it happened long before AIDS was a thing, but because he was such a great guy, I want to honor him with the distinction of infecting me.

I learned the basics of fisting by playing with men and being played with at the Catacombs, but my ass wasn't ready to take a hand; that would take a year. Michael had meaty hands that didn't collapse, so it was Dr. Harry Banghart, a small wiry man from a good family in Virginia, who fisted me for the first time in the playroom he converted from the open space in the attic.

Steve's death ended my time at the Catacombs. I was honored to be invited to join his family. At a time when a man could be fired and thrown out of his apartment for being queer, the Catacombs celebrated birthdays with sheet cakes smothered in icing.

The Hothouse on Fifth Street, south of Market, was the penultimate pleasure palace of sophisticated grit, the black plastic membership card an instant collector's item. Wakefield Poole, who produced the porno classics *Boys in the Sand* and *Bijou*, was the inspiration behind Hot Flash, the quirky in the most surprising ways general store on Upper Market. He needed a place to indulge his fantasies, so combining his ribald imagination with a crew of workers, an SRO hotel on 5th Street materialized as three stories of sexual gratification.

I checked in at the sidewalk. The centerpiece on the first floor was a giant twenty-by-twenty-foot hammock of black car tires and silver chains; at the lowest, it was two feet off the floor. A steamy hot Italian American Land a lithe gymnast play fighting nude in the hammock was the stuff of legends. The chain-link maze that no one used because men did not come to the Hothouse to just suck dick was masked with oat-colored canvas. Fire engine red lockers were stacked two high behind chain link fencing like a line of new recruits. The second I opened the top button of my Levis, I was Raw Recruit #1, and all eyes were on me. It was a test, am I man enough to expose my nakedness to a room of strangers?

The DJ pin lit from above worked a turntable on a platform two feet off the floor. When the DJ was Peter Fisk, the night was guaranteed to be high energy. The second floor was beige and so were the men who played there. They had sex. I wasn't satisfied with just having sex because there were ways of having sex more gratifying, so I was constantly experimenting.

There was a hierarchy in bathhouses. There were the players at the top who took the sport of sex seriously, the regulars, and a combination of the timid and those that went there so they could tell their friends they'd been there. I was a player.

My floor was the top floor. Painted entirely black, the only light on the floor was the neon green exit sign at the end of the hall, so it was dark, and the only sound was the moans and the "Ah fucks!" coming from the mouths of the men having sex.

I always got a room on the lightwell, and one night it paid off. Two men were having hot sex in the room across the lightwell. To spruce up our evenings with a shift in sex, I invited them to join me and Michael in our room. The combined sexual energy of hour men was remarkable and each of us made sure everyone was treated equally. That's phenomenal when you think about it. Wakefield changed the toys in his room on that floor all the time. He had an exam table with stirrups, a St. Andrew's cross, a parachute harness that he strung up in a corner, and whatever triggered his imagination that day at breakfast.

The corner room was the piece de résistance. The bay

windows were slivers of mirror, so when I was in the sling in the middle of the bay, I could see my ass from three sides as well as in the mirror above me. The room was reserved on weekends, so when I used it, I felt I'd broken a barrier. The only time I hopped in the sling was Tuesday. The man, a few years older than me with pale skin and a full head of hair was dressed in slacks and oxfords. He could easily have been in town for his mother's funeral, but he had a powerful pent-up need, and he was extraordinarily skilled at satisfying that need. I'd be surprised if we exchanged more than four words.

Wakefield closed the Hothouse in 1983 because he wanted to keep the men who enjoyed his creation from being infected by a strange disease that was killing gay men. Mayor Dianne Feinstein closed the baths in 1984 because she didn't approve of group sex.

With the onset of AIDS, the pickings were slim. Russ Libby hosted his first sling party in a small storefront off Polk Street. After that, The Sling was an old two-story apartment house on Natoma Street South of Market. Russ was the consummate host. When a man was out of his mind on speed and bleeding profusely, he jumped into action and the man was quickly taken to hospital.

One night I was at the top of the stairs and Robert Gallegos, who inspired Thom Gunn's "American Boy," saw me, and he threw me in a sling. Our chemistry was pitch-perfect, and our hot and heavy performance caught the eye of Albert, a sculpted leatherman from Germany. He wanted to see if I was as good as I looked. After I finished playing with Robert, my time with Albert was one for the record books because Albert excelled at pleasuring me. We played as equals.

Robert told me he was afraid of falling in love with me. We

remained a favorite playmate until a cripplingly disease killed him, but I still remember him a special friend. Albert is a regular at Folsom Weekend, as when he's in town, I say, "Hey!"

Carl Hack and Jeff Mauk around the beginning of this century were the next to respond to the need for a play space for fisters. It was a private party in their Hickory Street home. With a crew of eager volunteers, it took eighteen hours for Carl to convert the garage and his carpenter's workshop into an amazing play place with a room with six slings, a padded platform in a space to socialize, and a covered outdoor space to chill and smoke dope. If I needed to touch up, he provided a two-piece bathroom. Jeff did a buffet in the kitchen upstairs, and he kept it stocked with cold drinks and salty snacks throughout the night. I played with a man from Vancouver at an early party. He was a big brown-haired man with great equipment and talented hands that knew their way around my ass. I always looked for him at parties, and we eventually did play another time. I felt I was playing with a brother.

An invitation to their parties was a gold ticket, and I felt honored every time I received one. Carl's Rolodex was the modern-day equivalent of Samuel Steward's Stud File, so when I played at their parties, I was playing with some of the finest players from around the globe.

Carl had an Amish harness maker in his hometown in Lancaster Pennsylvania make a sling that was done so handsomely it became the gold standard for slings with those of us in Carl's orbit.

Meals are the finest way to renew friendships, and Carl and Jeff were consummate hosts. Their holiday potluck dinners were family times when I renewed friendships. The camaraderie of their family kept me strong.

Carl and Jeff continued San Francisco's fist tradition that started at the Catacombs in proud masculine style.

They moved to Palm Springs, and now live near my buds

Growing up in Wausau, group sex wasn't a thing. When I was playing at the baths, I was so involved in experiencing the sensations that I didn't think about their permanence. Then, I hear Steve is dead, and the Catacombs is gone. A pleasure palace so perfect I never dreamed it could happen was gone in a flash. It was a lesson in permanence; nothing lasts forever.

If history is any guide, once this pandemic is over, there will be play spaces for fisters because there will always be men who are interested in fisting. The newest generation's ingenuity will make their play spaces more tech savvier than the ones I played in, but they'd be damned fools if they don't have as many thrilling adventures as I had.

Travels with Charley

I traveled with two passports, my US passport and my fist identity. They got me to spaces I wouldn't have found without them because they were places of the mind. The best way to know a foreign city and its people is through the eyes of someone who lives there, but I knew a culture through the way a man who lived there responded to touch; I knew his insides, and the space where he lived was a guide to his culture.

London

With a heritage that includes William Quarles, who lived in Ufford, Northhamptonshire, England in 1420, my trips to England were trips to the homeland.

This trip to Europe was planned months before I met

Michael, so I was madly in love with him 8,000 miles away. My first night in London, I met Norman Scott at the Coleherne, a leather bar in West London. To impress me, the first thing he said was, "I know Jeremy Thorpe." Most people today won't know who he was, but it piqued my interest because I'd heard Jeremy Thorpe was a rising progressive politician, and I kept track of them because I hope that one of them would someday make a body politic that serves everyone equally, a politic where no one was better than anyone else. The hopes of youth,

Norman took me to a South Kensington flat that felt like the place he and Jeremy had their trysts because shortly after getting there, two older men walked in. I was not working for a mayor, so I had no political credentials if one of them was Jeremy, so all I knew of him was a brief introduction and a politician's handshake. I was not invited to join them drinking, smoking. Norman and I in an adjacent room lay on a bed in the dark next to each other, and I was pissed. When I went home with a man in San Francisco, he was excited to see me because he knew he would be treated with respect when we had sex. Norman didn't want to have sex with me, he wanted a sympathetic ear to listen to his grievances.

Sex is the dance that starts with chit chat, then moves to feeling each other out with words and watching body language. Beneath the surface, I got a sense of his desire, someone dumb enough to listen to him.

When the Jeremy Thorpe scandal made the news, I wondered if the man I went home with was the same man that Thorpe tried to murder, but he never signed his name on paper so there is no way to confirm it. Then recently watching *A Very English Scandal* with Hugh Grant on Netflix, Norman getting his national security card was the key to his being angry. That security card, something I'd never heard of, was what Norman went on about the night I lay there pissed. With that cleared up, I can say with absolute certainty that Norman Scott is the man in London that I did not have sex with on that trip.

I had to see theater when I was in Shakespeare's town, so I scanned the papers for a play I heard about with nudity, thereby killing two birds, theater, and nudity with one stone. I was stoked when Oh! Calcutta! was running. I hopped on the tube at Earls Court and rode it to the Leicester Square. A devilishly handsome young man at the box office in the theater's entrance sold me a ticket. His sly grin unbeknownst to me meant the ticket was front row center, and he had plans for me.

Until the musical production started, I did not know that he was the principal actor. Midway through a scene, he pulled me from the audience and coddled me in his lap. I was embarrassed being handled in an audience of strangers, but I did my awkward best playing along with him.

I met Michael Gould, an American nurse, on that trip, and we've been buds ever since. On another trip, in a classic twenties apartment block right out of an Agatha Christie murder mystery in South London, he inserted a catheter in my urethra. At first, the strangeness of the plastic tube hurt, but once it was in place, the sensation of gentle electricity throbbing deep in me was dreamlike.

On my last visit, Mike hosted a party at the single-family home he shares with his husband in North London. That night, I played with ten tall well-endowed uncut men two of whom made my ass sing, the makings of an urban legend.

Melbourne

Howard was one of those spur-of-the-moment connections that make travel worth the tedium of taking shoes off, hours stuck in the same airline seat, and eating pre-measured plane food. It was my first night in town, so I checked out the Laird before retiring to my room. The crowd had thinned, just a murmuring couple and an empty bar. I was about to chalk up the night to Nice Try when, off in a corner, I saw Howard. He was a large man with a full beard. I had to hug him. Our eyes met and intuitively we knew each other. After exchanging a few words, I was in his Mazda on the way to his terrace home. It was dark, so I don't remember the details, but I remember weathered shutters and original hardware. Jasmine scented night air wafting through floor-length terrace window.

He put a kettle for tea on a cast-iron stove, and while he waited for it to boil, I got ready in his well-appointed shower where everything worked perfectly.

One of the hazards of fisting is its many pieces, and they all must work together perfectly for the experience to be worth my cleaning out.

When I shut off the hot water, he presented me with a warm towel because that's what buds do for each other. I was thousands of miles from San Francisco, Michael was in the Glorious Bathhouse in the Sky and vast Pacific between me and home, but with Howard's hand on my shoulder and my head on his chest, I was home.

Howard's red-blond hair tumbled to his shoulders. His body was large with love handles and a fine layering of fur that he lived in comfortably. He was an eminently huggable Teddy bear. He said he was embarrassed about the size of his dick, but I thought it was fine, and it did its job perfectly. Like a fine wine, his ass had matured over the years.

Some guys started by poking my ass on a mission to mediocrity. Howard was a gentleman, so he knew how to warm me up nice and slow. There was certainty in his touch, and tension evaporated. As soon as our clothes were history, we couldn't touch fast enough, sloppy kisses all over the place, tongues darting in and out. We were standing, we were making a mess of his bed, we were on the floor, I was on the edge of the bed with his tongue in my clean ass.

He made sure my body was telling him it wanted to feel his hand before he greased his and put it far enough in for me to remember the incredible feeling of a hand in my ass and the sensations that radiate throughout me

After letting me rest, he went back, this time further, and once he got far enough to sense what I was capable of, he went all in. I'm stoned on his fine dope and poppers, so the details are hazy, but my memory of both of us doing an outstanding job of building friendship by taking care of each other's needs is crystal clear.

For hours we traded top and bottom as seasoned pros until dawn's pink lips kissed the horizon. My time with Howard was a time of mutual affection and being part of his life.

When he dropped me off at my hotel, I knew a Melbourne few men knew.

Stockholm

Two Swedes online invited to a fist party that was being held when I would be in Stockholm. I held to my excitement about their party when I screwed up directions and I had a taxi driver take me outside Hamburg when the hotel with a reservation was well within the city of Hamburg. The trip so far had been a disaster, and I was still smarting from that when I discovered the party was within walking distance from where I was staying. That picked up my feelings, Stockholm with the hot men I met online was going to be a fun evening. With high hopes, I marched to the bar.

I knew the minute I walked through the heavy black oak doors this evening was not going to end well. The bar was empty and there were no signs of a fist party. A small group of friends still dressed for work stood talking quietly. By the time the couple that invited me showed up, I was trapped in an Ingmar Bergman movie. Around eleven, there were fifteen men in the bar, and it looked like they were dressed for a dinner club, and no one was having sex. There wasn't the ether of excitement in the air in the sex parties I knew in San Francisco. I'm impatient around sex, and I couldn't just sit on my hands, so I took the initiative. I put one man who invited me in a sling. I did a serviceable job fisting him, and he enjoyed it, but as far as his partner and everyone else in the bar was concerned, we were a just Gravad lax, a Swedish a piece of smoked salmon on top of a slice of dark bread

I have been in the game long enough to know rejection; it comes with the territory, and you learn to deal with it. But indifference? Sex for me was the most intimate human interaction, and one of the finest aspects of the human experience. Gay men I knew, and I knew hundreds of gay men, but they never behaved like that at a fist party. It was like fisting in the middle of an accountants' annual meeting. They were a puzzlement. Unlike so many of my passions, fisting energized as nothing else did. The feeling of a hand in me did something that nothing else did which is why I kept wanting a hand. No matter how long or how hard I played, and I was always ready for more. The nights I walked home in the wee hours at peace with the craziness in my life are some of my fondest memories.

I am Pisces, so I sense thoughts, and I have a stellar history. I wanted to know what made the men act the way they did that was so different from every group of gay men I knew, but I was so discouraged by their indifference, I just wanted to sleep it off.

I don't write off gay men because we all have value, but that night I was so pissed, I came close.

Holland

Amsterdam is a city of canals, tulips, and hung uncut men, and I've been there several times. This time, it was my first night in town, so I started at the pot café I knew just over one of its bridges, just wide enough for a car. In dim light, I was letting the pot set in when I was distracted by a straight dude who was trying to impress his date with how much he knew about pot. He was corporate and she Junior League. I couldn't stop laughing at his deflated ego when she flashed a giant pot brownie. Just as I got up to leave nicely stoned, I couldn't take my eyes off the couple right out of Central Casting for a Fellini movie about love.

I met Ivan Tse, a brilliant mind, at a play party in 1986. He is six feet tall, and his lithe body had just enough muscle in just the right places to make it perfectly proportioned. I knew from his first word that he was a responsible adult, so I could relax and enjoy the show. From what he told me, he doesn't have a lot of sex, but that that night, he showed me he'd been trained well. Once naked and touching, play started at an elevated level of eroticism, and he kept it there using the best of what he learned from the finest guides to give me a regal journey of pleasures

Our play ended at just the right time because both of us knew we should stay healthy and get a good night's sleep. Our connection began a friendship that's lasted thirty years. His family's charitable foundation even made a gift to the library campaign.

On my last visit to Amsterdam in 2001, Ivan took me to a nude health club in Amsterdam. The large industrial-style building was well built, far from Dam Square. Compared to the narrow canal houses with steep, winding staircases, it was an open and airy structure. I was impressed with the Dutch's concern for healthy living. I felt clean being there.

Half was a large open dining hall where I dined on a perfectly prepared filet of sole. The other half was devoted to healing with multiple hot tubs, a well-appointed sauna, and a handsome steam room. We went our separate ways, and I relieved stress in a hot tub at one of the saunas.

When I asked Ivan if I could use his name in this memoir, he was living in Hong Kong, where he is now president of his family's global business.

In 1999, I was in Holland for a day before jumping across the Channel to London and from Heathrow the next day boarding a flight back to San Francisco. It was autumn, and it got dark earlier because Amsterdam is further north than San Francisco. In the darkness I was a trench-coat detective in search of a hearty meal.

The day instead of being a day of soothing relief from the disastrous time I just had in Stockholm I desperately needed, it was just a day. The trams ran on time and traffic stopped while a bridge was raised. No one cared about my need to be touched.

Before I went out for dinner on a cold, damp night, I scanned the profiles on a fisting website. A man's face caught my attention, but I passed because he identified himself as a bottom. I appreciated his honesty because it made my night simpler. He wanted one thing, and I wanted something else.

The peanut-infused Indonesian meal in a tiny canal-side restaurant was now well in my system and the hour was late. I wanted sex; that's the reason I booked a room at the Black Tulip. I wanted to cap off the miserable time in Stockholm with a vigorous fist session.

I ran through the profiles again. This time I read what the bottom said about himself, and he sounded like a decent human being. Truth be told, my standards have a way of slipping when my libido's in charge, so this time I thought he was worth a shot. He replied instantly, which meant he was either hot to trot, or he was fucked out of his mind on speed. I was horny, so I risked it.

A dark shadow knocked on my window as a canal boat sloshed against a buoy. I knew him only by his profile face, and I had more urgent things to do than ask him to sign his name on a piece of paper, so I do not know his name.

Once inside and free of Dutch dampness that slithers up your spine like a frozen monkey, we dispensed with small talk. In our rush to get started, shirts and jeans flew off, boots kicked off.

His build was strong, with tasty bits of brown on his chest, and an inviting happy trail drew me to his nicely packaged uncut dick and balls. The heat between us rose, but his dark eyes revealed nothing. His square head looked German, but he was a Brit. We were about the same age, which is the way I like my men.

It was late, so we wasted no time getting down to the business at hand, his ass. Right off the bat, I let him know that his ass would be cared for, and knowing that, I his hole got ready for a fantastic ride.

He was unapologetic about what he wanted, and he trusted that I would take care of his ready hole. There wasn't a thing that my arm or my fist did, and I was on my A-game, that he wanted me to do more forcefully.

He was surprised at my ability to take him to the stratosphere and keep him there. Keeping him at peak took years of experience, and there's nothing that gets my dick harder than feeling an ass trembling around my hand as I speed up, slow down, and speed up as long as he can take it.

His getting off on what I was doing, evidenced by his smooth, elastic hole, inspired me to take him as far as he could take my hand and then see if he could take more which is exactly what he wanted. We repeatedly egged each other on getting my hand deeper and deeper into him, but that was not enough.

We were swirling in the sea of ecstasy, but we needed more. After a quick espresso and joint, I got down to fisting him with even greater intensity using a technique I learned from Jeff Bosacki. I slowly and methodically loosened his ass so it could get my hand far into him, and when he let me get further, I circled his second ring with my index finger.

I pulled out and I let him take a breather. Once he was rested, he took a hit of poppers, and I started by popping my hand in and out, and the more I popped his ass, the looser he got, but he still wanted more. I had a dancing bear on my arm.

A health note. Ass skin is resilient, but it was also fragile, so there is a difference between a loose hole like the Brit's and a sloppy hole. A sloppy hole is he hole of a man on drugs. The Brit respected his hole, and he took care of it, so even when it was loose enough to make a popping sound, his hole had enough training to take it without it being damaged. Drugs shut down controls, so men on drugs have a higher rate of tearing skin and bleeding profusely. Playing with a sloppy hole I felt sorry for the guy because he missed one of the great joys of being a gay man.

At two AM, I asked him to fist me, not something I ask bottoms because bottoms bottom. To reward me for giving him two rounds of perfect pleasure, he said. "Let's do it." My circuits shot into overdrive. I had just had two tumultuous rounds, but years taught me to keep a smidgen in reserve. I wanted to make the most of his gift, and with that reserve, I could give him my A-game.

When he started, I was already turned on by his stellar performances, so I was going to show him my A-game. His years of experience paid off because being a bottom gave him an intimate knowledge of what pleasures a man's ass. He knew how to find the places that opened me further and those that had me closing my eyes and soaring into a world of flashing colors and floating creatures.

Our symbiosis was natural, and the feeling was ecstasy on an elevated level with my body a swarming mass of Technicolor pleasures.

We finally wore each other out at four AM. He said he'd shower when he got back to where he was staying. As we stood at the door with canal cold worming its way through my feet, I could tell by the way he hugged me that I gave him what he desperately needed.

His saying, "You surprised me," reminded me I was doing the work of the fisting gods.

Hanging up My Spurs

Fisting, like all forms of dating, was rough and tumble. Tender human emotions played off each other, as I tried to find stability and a level of comfort. In my forty-year career, there was competition, there was stupidity, and there was mind-blowing sex. With Michael the most intimate moment was when exhausted from sex we lay next to each other, our bodies talking to each other.

My goal were moments of intimacy, so someone had to lead, and someone had to follow, and because tender parts were exposed, those roles had to stay the same until they changed and stayed the same.

I got messed up when I gave mixed signals because they confused them, and I was this big shot city planner that worked for the mayor. I had to be clear with them.

Michael and I, both Pisces, didn't need direction, we instinctively knew what to do.

And then there's the godfather abandonment issues, so nothing hurts me more deeply than when I feel someone has rejected me because it means they don't love me. I went into funks, I was inadequate. Over time tough skin built. I didn't like being rejected, but I tried to think of his reasons beyond the old standby of he-doesn't-like me. Maybe he had terrible day at work and needed quiet time, or maybe something I never thought of. Knowing most men don't see through the lens of sex that I do helped. Seeing him as human set my feelings aside.

That was not as easy as it sounds because rejection runs deep, and when my feelings were set aside, they were still there, so when I was rejected the next time, I had to repeat the process of setting it aside, in a never-ending dance.

What I learned about human kindness as a Unitarian Universalists was the warm place that I returned to when I'd been rejected. I closed my eyes and looked at myself and after I felt sorry for myself for a while, feeling rejected was a waste of time.

Nothing is more important to me than friends, human and canine. They keep me strong, and friendships made in those forty years with the men still alive and some dead are among my deepest friendships. I don't know feel the same with men that I haven't had sex with.

I hurt people. I know that, and didn't apologize to them, and I ask them to forgive me.

My optimism about the future was battered by Donald J. Trump and his cronies' attempts to undermine democracy because I cherish our democracy because it gave me this life. I continue being political because I believe it's my responsibility as a citizen to participate in the political process. It is ugly and nasty but it's still the best form of government that humankind has created so far. Since the day I came out in California I keep on fulfilling my dream.

I didn't know what an immune system was until AIDS. One of the reasons, besides my genes, that I have lived this Long is my health regime. I've been doing acupuncture for thirty years, and it's kept my energies in balance. Ed Lee, the straight man I see in Santa Rosa who grew up in a commune besides being my acupuncturist, is also my therapist.

I've been ingesting a Chinese herb formulation that supports my immune system ever since I started taking AIDS meds, and all but one of the many AIDS meds taken over the years has worked without side effects.

I have been collaborating with my trainer, David Ames, a former bodybuilder and song and dance man and all-around nice guy for ten years. He cares about my physical and my mental health twice a week.

I've always had dogs, and Charley and Stonewall's loyalty and love have enriched my life as a single man. I couldn't do it with a dog. They pulled me through during lockdown. Stonewall is at my side when I wake in the morning.

Today I am double boosted, and this is my second pandemic, and so far, I've survived both, but Covid gets more transmissible with every newscast.

I wanted long ago to be in the center of the action, and I did that bigtime.

My time as a fister is over, and it's time to look back at my career. Why did I devote forty years to fist fucking? Isn't there a better way to spend time than with a man's hand in my butt?

The short answer is there's nothing like it; the experience of a hand in my ass is the most intimate connection I can have with a man. It's unlike any other feeling, it's a carnival of happiness.

Fisting combined my twin fascinations: the male body and touch. I was not just gliding my hand over his thighs and exciting his ass, my fingertips got within a whisker of his beating heart. I knew a man's body when I saw him naked, and when he let me put my hand in him, I knew that more about him.

It hurt like hell! For me to take a hand, I had to be counterintuitive because ass muscles are designed to keep shit in the body, and I had to train those muscles to ignore the factory-installed program and learn how to accept a well-lubricated hand being slid into it. The closest comparison is childbirth.

Think of the anus as the Strait of Hormuz, the bottleneck between the Persian Gulf and the Gulf of Oman. The anus is the bottleneck between the external sphincter muscle and the internal rectum. Getting his hand through a clean anus hurt like hell because the anus that was programmed to contract was being told to do the opposite and be stretched to its limits. When his hand got past the clean anus, it was in my rectum, and that is lined with excitable receptors, and when they were excited by his hand, they send rings of ecstasy radiating throughout me.

The lasting pleasure reward of his hand in me far outweighed the brief pain. Some pain reminds me I'm alive.

Would I do it again? Do the fabulous times with a few men make up for the times that weren't so fabulous? Does one fantastic fuck mean that much? Fisting is a mutual exchange, and I did it in ways that made it both emotionally and physically rewarding for me. The feeling of utter relaxation is unique to fisting.

My connection with buds like Jeff Bosacki and Richard Street was a soul connection, and I have never experienced anything like it with other men. That I write about them shows how essential they are to me.

Also, and this is a big also, there's no reason to believe that men in another life would be more talented or more fun to play with than the men I played with over the course of my forty-year career. I can't imagine finer teachers and playmates. The Universe did an excellent job proving me with the best coaches.

I thank my buds who are alive, as well as those who have passed on, for their generosity of spirit. You all did an excellent job taking care of my needs.

Rusty Dragon
In Memoriam

Red-head Rusty Dragon had the body of a gymnast and the soul of a mischievous angel. He was my hero the first time I saw him when he and his lover, Peter Fisk on the front page of the *Bay Area Reporter*. The picture of them was taken at the Night Flight Party, the city's first large-scale disco party. I thought him delicious and oh so fuckable.

The next time I saw him up, was at my first fist party in a private home, a big house in the western part of the city. Hugo Neihaus, who was completely and utterly into fisting, took me to the party. I was on the floor of the living room and because I was amazed to be at such a party, I have no memory what I drug I was on. Rusty and Peter showed up and they became the instant stars of the party. Both were trim and muscular with Rusty's body covered with freckles. Watching them fist was watching the gods at play. What I remember about that party was that he wasn't clean, and he had to step away and get clean, and everyone took in stride. That blew me away. Peter and Rusty only played with each other, and they were madly in love.

The next time I saw him was when I stumbled on him and Peter and two of their friends at the Geysers on a hot July day. I never expected to see him there, and I was shocked when he asked me to join them. When standing on top of a boulder at a bend in the river, Rusty offered me a joint laced with a white substance. I couldn't believe his ease in the way he accepted me because I considered Peter gay aristocracy and far above me. I'd never been treated like that. After a tasty meal that Peter made over a campfire, we sat in a circle around the fire. Peter took a steel ball bearing the size of an eight ball from Rusty's clean ass, put it in his mouth and the ball passed around the circle mouth to mouth. I thought that was so cool. Being the group's novice, they gave me a pass when I bungled taking the ball when it was passed to me.

The next time I saw Rusty he was part of the crew that worked at Hot Flash, the glorious consequence of Wakefield Poole's vivid imagination. Wakefield directed porno movies *Bijou* and *Boys in the Sand*. The Hothouse was also his creation. Hot Flash was a once in a lifetime light airy store on upper Market with painted mail on the floor of the front door so realistic, I bent to pick it up. The store had the most outrageous collection of housewares, and a leaping tiger circus poster covered one wall. For the holidays, every surface in the store had a bromeliad in all their wild and crazy forms when most people didn't know what a bromeliad was. To show how radical they were, Rusty and the entire staff shaved their heads.

I was excited every time I played with Rusty at the Hot

House because he was so easy to play with. He was a sponge of joy and he excited me naturally. He was generous with his body which meant I was touching a god when I played with him. Every time we played, I was utterly relaxed because he was a master of the art of fisting, and he could do anything he wanted to do. Every time we played was a special treat and I left feeling good about me.

The AIDS epidemic struck, and I heard Peter died. As the epidemic growled on, and I heard nothing about Rusty. Then after the epidemic subsided, I ran into him outside the Safeway in Rincon Center. I was surprised to see him, and he remembered me. He'd lost his boyish charm, but his beautiful soul glowed behind his smile, and his body still had the shape it had when I saw him at the Geysers. I don't get how some men never lose their teenage physique. Knowing he was alive gave me hope for the future.

With that, I thought the Universe gave me closure, and then I heard he died.

I lost so many friends who loved me to AIDS, and they should be alive today.

Rusty epitomized everything joyous about that time, and his end is a fitting end to that time.

California Dreaming

AIDS left sorrow in its wake, and I needed a fresh start. I had to have a one-story home because I expected to live there until I left for the Glorious Bathhouse in the Sky. I'd already added an elevator to the three-flat Edwardian in San Francisco in anticipation of being old and unable to climb the fifty-six steps to the third floor. Flat wanted a writing cubbyhole with Comcast because the Internet is essential.

My first editor, Michael Samuel, has a home with his husband in Occidental, and he knew a realtor in Sebastopol. Rochelle Continente, who was with Michael when he died, lived in Sebastopol. The property in Sebastopol I ended up buying has two acres and a three-bedroom home equipped with gas and Comcast. The second building has a two-room apartment, a two-car garage, and a spare room. The artfully crafted garden is drought tolerant, the Harold and Maude settee is nestled beneath an arbor of ancient grape vines, and there's an open field at the back of the property. The large chain link enclosure was designed for dogs.

The prior owner, a lesbian screenwriter, used the apartment in the second building as her writing studio. My writing cubbyhole was her dining room.

The view from the deck of the valley is spectacular.

When I saw the garden, I told the realtor, "I have a brown thumb, and there's no way in hell I'm going to take care of it." He assured me a woman took care of everything. Once I was on the property, she turned out to be a landscape architect who charged more than dinner for a family of five at a five-star restaurant, so for years, the garden languished. A gay man saved it in 2019, and he's bought it back to its former glory, adding plants that gives it a broader spectrum of species. The bulbs bought every year add splashes of color.

My first tenant grew pot he enclosed by covering the fencing in the back of the property with black plastic sheets. He showed me papers from the county permitting him to grow pot for personal health reasons, but who really believes that?

I make every place I own my own. This home was move-in ready, but I knew from the start that the kitchen with a Sub-Zero refrigerator and Wolf range that stopped working wasn't designed by someone who cooks, and I didn't know why a previous owned added two strange rooms with a fold down ironing board and a toilet. Who does that much ironing and pissing?

As a property owner, and I can't do it without a general contractor, and once I have a great one, I held on to him. Tall, blond Steve Alberts did all the work on my home in Calaveras County. He confided as a teenager; he'd drop out of school so he could fuck women in a commune. He asked me how I used a cock ring. There was always one mistake with his work, but he liked each other and was quick to respond to my requests.

The general contractor who did the elevator in the three-flat Edwardian in San Fransisco did not supervise his old guy electrician who, without telling me, worked on his own schedule leaving a trail of plaster and plaster dust wherever he went. The flat was unlivable until he finished. An eight-piece set of French silverware and a collection of state quarters were stolen by one of his helpers.

David Jursic did the shower room in San Franisco. He' a Croat, dependable outstanding work. He's one of my best friends, and he talks about his family, and we agonize over the political catastrophe. Frank did the initial work on the house in Sebastopol, but he stopped working when contractors were hard to find because they were rebuilding the neighborhoods destroyed by wildfires. David bailed me out, and he has done all the work around the house ever since and he is now replacing the deck. A local artist who makes sculptures from found objects made me a sculpture of with me and two dogs in a VW Microbus that stands at the entrance.

I must not give off gay vibes around my contractors because both were amazed that I was an outspoken liberal. When he heard I voted for a Democrat, Frank stopped working for me

After Dad died, I had money to convert the awkward kitchen and the two useless adjacent rooms into a chef's kitchen with a farm sink, quartz countertops and cherry wood cabinets. I moved the washer and dryer from the useless rooms to a new space off the kitchen in space I took from the garage because I only have one car. Sliding barn doors keep them out of sight.

David replaced the outdated double sinks and shower room in the ensuite with the double sink I had to buy when I saw it at Pottery Barn. He did the hex tile shower room with a bench that honor's the hex tile shower room in the city.

David turned one of the two garages in the second building into a writing studio. My original intention was to make it available to queer writers at no cost so they could finish a book, and a talented young writer selected by the Lambda Literary Foundation used it before Covid struck. Now it's a guest room that's been used by a first responder, Trebor Healey, and David Penner used it during his three weeks here.

Over the years, I had to replace the holding tank, the heating and air conditioning, and a large section of the driveway.

When David Penner moved to Canada, I found Nido through a friend of David's. He is also a Croat, and he is recovering from an unhappy marriage. He's a natural with plants and he is doing an excellent job caring for the chickens who produce more eggs than they did when David cared for them. Because he takes care of the chickens and the garden in the lower half of the property, and he puts the trash out for pickup and walks the dogs he pays no rent. He's worth it because he takes the burden off me.

I'm starting to believe, with him and David coming here after disastrous marriages, that unintentionally, I made the property The Forester Home of Recovering Gay Husbands.

Initially, I saw the apartment in the second building as a place for the domestic partner from hell because it was far enough from the main house. If he were in my life, he would be at a distance. He has a PhD in herpetology, and our relationship went south six months after he moved to San Francisco, but I kept hoping he would pull it together. Eventually, I'd had enough of him not pulling it together, and I terminated the relationship before I signed the papers on the property. He disappeared, and I have no idea where he is.

Food is an essential part of life in Sonoma County, and Sebastopol has not forgotten its hippie roots. The tie-dyed shirt at Goodwill had many lives, Screamin' Mimi's Ice Cream has a line around the corner, and a mayor ran a pot dispensary. Everyone goes about their business, and they let me get through a line of traffic so I can turn into the Safeway parking lot. I can park on Main Street, and I never drive congested streets because I know the backroads. I can get to the family owned Fircrest Market, my steady date for food and household goods where I'm known as a regular, three separate ways. Most roads in the county are not heavily traveled which makes getting around a lot less stressful than it is getting around in the city.

I stopped going to the city every month to collect rent checks. Alejandro, an Argentine friend of David Penner, lives in the Edwardian flat that Michael and I made home, and he pays minimal rent because he is the manager of the building, giving him the sweetest deal in San Francisco's ridiculously expensive housing market. He brings me the rent checks and my mail in the city every month. He's a dog walker, so when he comes, he brings his dog Shaggy, a poodle mix, and the dog in his care. For my pooches, his visits are Christmas. They go wild sniffing butts and chasing each other around the property.

I used the Sunday farmers market in the center of town to see get acquainted with Sebastopol's oddities, but mostly it's aging hippies and young couples eager to get the freshest produce for the week and a gift for a newborn's first birthday. The star attraction is the man who makes paella. You must get there early and there's always a line.

Life is in the country is restful. My neighbors work and live on their farms, no agribusiness here. The two apple trees and a plum tree in spring when they are in bloom are spectacular.

Mighty oaks line one edge of the property. Six redwoods and twelve white birch trees stand guard in front of the house. I feel close to the earth when I'm on the property.

Sebastopol is particular about its growth and its businesses. The only fast food in town is the one McDonald's on the road out of town and a Papa John's Pizza joint tucked in a mini mall on another road out of town. No building is taller than three stories. A recent multiuse development was scratched, and the city lost population in the last census. The local Rialto Cinema, one of the largest in the county, has hip taste, and they go all out for Pride. There are fine restaurants like the linen table up to speed with the latest food trend restaurants like The Farmer's Wife in the Barlow, an innovative Thai restaurant tries new takes on Asian cuisines, and there's a burger joint that's been around forever, and an order of fries is big enough to feed a regiment. In addition to the Fircrest Market, there's Whole Foods, Safeway, Lucky, and Pacific Market. The box stores, Costco, Best Buy, Trader Joes, and the rest along with cheap gas are nine miles away in Santa Rosa.

The cultural events and activities in the *Bohemian*, our hip free paper, fill two pages. The Sebastopol Art Museum sponsors an annual open studio that has local jewelry makers, sculptors, painters, potters, painters, and clothing makers open their studio, and folk come from miles around to see what they made and sometimes buy something. The Art Museum is open all year with classes. I added to my art collection from both.

Pot is legal in California, and I was interested to see it affected life in Sebastopol. It's become so regular; I didn't notice any change.

I have always had standard poodles because, unlike most dogs that have fur, poodles have hair, so they are hypo allergenic. They are also the most intelligent dogs. Getting these two chocolates started with me in the parking lot of a Walmart in Tracey, halfway between the breeder in the Sierras and me. I was on the phone to her, and she was telling me where she was but that was not nearby. We went back and forth for an hour with me being increasingly pissed at her because she was not making sense. It was blistering hot, and my phone battery died. Disgusted, I drove the metered highspeed lanes to get back to sanity as fast as I could. I sent her an email expressing my frustration at her stupidity. She responded by apologizing and said she would bring her dogs to me.

Three days later, she showed up with a van with six dogs in cages on a hot September day. I pitied the poor dogs cramped in their small metal cages in the sweltering heat; she left the doors of the van open. I had the choice of three males with tails. I chose one of the two cuddlers, Charley, and the loner, Stonewall.

She asked if I really wanted two twelve-week-old puppies. With fenced property for them to run and they'd be happier with a brother, I took both. I've had dogs all my life, but I wasn't ready for them. They destroyed four chairs and two couches in the country and the city, they ruined three rugs beyond redemption, and some furniture still has marks of their teeth. Until recently, I had an ongoing saga of them running away. Stonewall is the ringleader, and Charley, his Morgan Freeman companion. They ate through the lattice work under the deck and knew how to get under the fence on the side of the yard. When they run at forty-five miles an hour, there is no stopping them. I had a fence built high enough to keep them in one the side of the backyard, and just soon as the fence was in place, they got out. I built a twenty-foot fence of redwood that ain't cheap in another area, and the second it was in place, they were gone. They ran away nine times, and they are the reason I know a fair amount of the surrounding county. Once I had to drive ten miles to pick them up, and they slept far from home overnight twice.

Neighbors are exceedingly kind and concerned about animals' wellbeing, so after a while, when they ran away, rather than trying to find them, I just waited for the phone call. Stonewall is now on a sixty-foot leash. My hand is firm but gentle so he knows I'm not going to hurt him, but he can't get away when I take him to the leash. Charley's the old guy, and Stonewall's a love beside me when I wake in the morning.

I've just begun getting involved with the Senior Center. I was surprised at the impressive clean building with multiple rooms and what will soon have thanks to a successful capital campaign a state-of-the-art kitchen. It's the real deal. The two meals for ten dollars I ate there were outstanding, and the Covid-19 lockdown had the center delivering thousands of meals to the homebound. I am learning tai chi there.

It is run as a professional nonprofit, so feel comfortable being a donor. This year, I was offered riding in the Center's vehicle in the Sonoma County Pride parade. I feel comfortable as an old guy there.

Homes and how people live in them fascinate me, so I get regular postings of homes for sale, and Sebastopol has an identifiable home style. The fascination began when Mom drove me in a black 1947 Oldsmobile along Lake Drive in Milwaukee in the early fifties. As the Gothic stone mansions flew by, I saw me in one of the mansions because I hated being young, and they represented adult, the center of action where I knew I would be happy.

Masseurs in Sonoma County were rare, and the two I saw weren't doing it for me. In 2015, a round, blond face popped up on a massage website. I didn't recognize his style, but I was desperate. I needed to be touched so I contacted him immediately. To show how jaded I'd become, my first impression of tall, blond David Penner was that he is an upbeat decent man.

Before the first massage, he asked if I minded if he smoked dope. Hallelujah! I love being stoned because the brain is the most crucial element in processing touch, and I'm in my head when I'm stoned. Both of us stoned was part of David's massages for sex years.

I told the tenant in the second building I knew he was growing more pot than the legal limit. Overnight, he disappeared. David was living on his own for the first time, having recently divorced his husband. I offered the apartment to him. The lower section of the property had that apartment, a vacant space, and the chain-link enclosure. David used the enclosure for chickens. I let him use the vacant space for his massage studio.

I was excited he is going to on the property one hundred feet from my house, so I went overboard on a shopping spree at Bed, Bath & Beyond to make sure his kitchen had everything a chef's kitchen had. We left the store with a shopping cart packed to the gills with chef's knives, sturdy pots, a set of dinner plates, bowls, scads of utensils, tea towels, a peppermill, a drying rack, the whole Julia Child. Once David was on the property, I began to appreciate the garden because I spent more time in it, and now I meditate under the grape arbor with the *Harold and Maude* settee.

Gay men hire masseurs for various reasons. One man I imagine had enough of the passive-aggressive boyfriend that he can't get rid of, and he wants to forget the whole thing and finds a masseur on the Internet. I imagine another wants to stop debating should I wear the powder blue polo shirt or the Lucy shirt to the next party? He never misses a party, sometimes leaving with boyfriends that never last. When he's looking for the date of the next White Party in Palm Springs, but hits the wrong key, and gets a massage website.

I'm a touch junkie, and I like nothing better than being touched by a man.

Massages are different. I've had a host of massage styles, from Swedish with long strokes, to tantric, an ancient mystical practice, and everything in between. David's massages are sensuous; they are spiritual sex.

He worked on my body for six years and knew what he was looking for and he exploited my hot spots and the releases I didn't know were there. He's been perfecting his touch for so long that his touch is sure and gentle with just the right amount of pressure, the mark of a true artist.

He caresses every part of me, making love to certain parts, and then he moves on to the next part. There isn't a part of me where he hasn't been able to drive me crazy because he knows the touch that does that. My ass has been touched by thousands of hands, and it has a reputation to uphold. David respects its reputation and gives it special attention that over time got more complex because from what his hands told him he knew more

I stored muscle memories in my thighs and ass in the seventies, and he knows where they are. When he goes there, I am having sex with Rusty Dragon at the Hothouse. What he does feels exactly what I remember what it felt like when I was having sex with Rusty at the Hothouse. He also penetrates me as special treats, but it's not my ass or mouth.

David was here for three weeks, and during the four massages while he was here, I returned to Nirvana. I carried resentment from him calling me a sexual predator. I told him that before the first massage, and he turned it back on me. With that, I'd had enough of the routine. because it was a waste of time, I dropped resentment halfway through the massage. The second massage it was gone. The next massage was the best sex I've had in years.

The journey began with him working my torso with slow steady motions that built in intensity, and when he lay his chest on my back, the energy peaked, and for a second our energies exchanged. It felt like cumming. That instant flashed me back to the day I was standing nude ankle deep in the Navarro River in Sonoma County. With my first psilocybin mushroom coursing through my blood, I'd just made love to my first boyfriend, ruggedly handsome Clay Grillo on the sleeping bags in our campsite.

I see him downstream, and I reach to the sun declaring, "This is the best day of my life!"

That instant was the start of my life as the man I am today. Up until that then, I was using material from the Gay Man 101 course in the air. David's last massage was more somber because he was leaving the next day, and neither of us is big on being open with our emotions, but he sent me off with one of his bone shattering moves

After one of David's massages, I was stoned as I climbed the incline from the massage studio to the house. I stood in the driveway, and I took it all in. I spread my arms and took in my home and the redwood guarding the gate and the sky above me. As I look around, I think, "Damn, you did it, Forester!"

On those cold, lonely nights with my family in expensive ruins, I never thought I would be a writer and living in the perfect home on two beautifully landscaped acres in Sonoma

County, California. I devoted my life to strengthening the lives of my queer brothers and sisters. I was loved unconditionally for eighteen years by a remarkable man. I had a successful forty-year career as a sexual athlete. I am slow now, but I am very much alive at seventy-eight. I did it.

My history with massage started when I came out in 1972. Those were years in San Francisco when there was a tremendous amount of sex, and my massages included dicks sucked, dicks jacked, and holes penetrated in a joyous frenzy of communal eros. The gay masseurs I worked with before I was living with Michael were young and not afraid of the body. That's more important than you think because a lot of men fear their body due to ancient bans on body touching. For some, body touching was a prelude to premarital sex, and for others it was the slippery slope to the final destruction of the fabric of Christian civilization. In the early days, when I put my hand on a man's ass, it might not be a regular occurrence for him because few men had touched his ass, it was virgin territory.

I started by exploring it with my hands to get a sense of it, and once I sensed how receptive he was, I increased the intensity. I can't describe exactly what I did because it was instinctual, and it was what it was at that moment. Most men liked having their ass played with, there's something basic about that feeling.

After Michael died, sex became a regular part of the massage with two masseurs. I met Paul online, and our sex was so ferocious I thought I'd found another life partner, but he was seeing a mysterious man. Sex energized him, so sex became so consistent that we both looked forward to having sex during the next massage. The other is well known, so he remains anonymous. I saw him off and on as he moved away and then moved back. When he started, he said his massages were non-sexual. Years later, he surprised me. It caught me off guard. After that, somewhere during a massage he switched the massage to sex. He got off on sex with me as much as I did; it was a release for him.

David left in November last year to care for his mother in Vanderhoof who suffers from Alzheimer's disease. He came back for three weeks in May 2022.

He grew up in a Mennonite family in Vanderhoof, British Columbia, and he is the only sibling of ten siblings to leave Vanderhoof; the rest of his family still lives in Vanderhoff. He has a straight twin, and until he was ten, his father called David "Twin." That must rip apart your self-confidence.

While here, he became an American citizen. He made friends and he composed and read his poetry.

At first, a submerged urge to be loved in me saw David as a long-term partner, but he wanted someone closer to his age. When I thought about what a long-term relationship involved, I was not ready for that. I couldn't risk another heartbreak. Besides, relationships are a shitload of work and take an enormous amount of energy. The ninety minutes on his table was our time of shared sensuality.

David's massages are more rewarding than sex was because they energize my spirit in ways that sex never did. Massage is mess-free while sex is a greasy mess that takes hours to clean up.

During the year of lockdown, David was the complete companion. We made meals together, we went to Costco together, and riding shotgun as he drove the backroads of the county, I got to know the county I was coming to love. Sonoma is an agricultural county with small farms and vineyards and families that have lived on them for generations, and that sense of continuity was comforting when elsewhere in the world, people were locked in their homes, filling hospital beds to capacity and trying to stay alive on ventilators. Many died. We were scrupulous about cleanliness, so while we continued massages, the property remained virus free.

Being wealthy was foisted on me, and while that doesn't sound so bad, it meant trying to be authentic while being constantly aware that I have more than most people have. It set me apart from the kids in school in Wausau.

I gave David a rototiller that he could use to improve the property, and he thought I expected sex in return. I knew his husband cheated but emotions are a confounding mystery, so I won't speculate on why sex was such a trigger for him.

David was brought up in a home where the only book in the house was the Bible, so sex means something different to him. Once the idea of my being sexually active was lodged in his mind, there was nothing I could do or say that would dislodge it. We had knock down drag out arguments over it that I don't like; it's a miserable way to communicate with someone you love.

Over a year ago, after a massage, I'm stoned, and as I climb the incline from the massage studio to the house. I stand in the drive, and I take it in. I take in my home and the redwood guarding the gate and the sky above me. As I look around me, I think, "Damn, you did it, Forester!"

David left in November to care for his mother in Vanderhoof who suffers from Alzheimer's Disease. With David gone, I separated my feelings for him, and I stopped subsidizing him. Before he came the last time, I didn't tell him that I was going to wait and see if he had changed when he came back. I should have told him.

His visit was a short trip, and he lined up more clients than he expected. Four were further than his Vespa could take him. This was my chance to let him know our relationship changed. I sent him an email asking him which table he was going to use. He assumed I gave him the table and he raced to the house wondering what was going on. I asked him again, "Which table are you taking?" He confessed he was planning to take the one I bought for the massage studio. I asked, "Have you asked me?" I saw the bolt of recognition on his face, our relationship had changed. He asked if he could use the table, and I agreed with him promising he would take care of it.

I had a tough time relaxing during his first massage because I still resented him for calling me a sexual predator. When I told him that at the beginning of the massage, he turned it back on me. Once I voiced it, I'd had enough of the sad routine. Halfway through the massage I was enjoying the massage the way I've always enjoyed his massages. During the second massage the resentment was gone. His last massage was the best sex I've had in years.

I thought that was our last massage, but he told me he was going to give me a massage for my letting him use the table.

Our last massage had a serious tone. We knew it was the last time we were going to be together, and he wanted to keep it controlled. Most of the ninety minutes was a time of moves he did regularly with his usual amazing touch, but toward the end he did something to my shoulders he'd never done before that took me back to a place I'd hid years ago because it hurt so much. He was doing something new, and I opened to him. I don't know where it was, but something in me opened.

We didn't have to say much with our farewells because we already knew what the other was thinking, and he was not big on displays of affection. He was going back to a job as manager of an apartment complex. It didn't pay well, but they were giving him a three-room apartment. That might be perfect if his parents decide they are too old to stay in the house that they've lived in their entire married lives. He said he was planning to come back in March of next year because school will be out, do guess there won't be much business in the building.

He changed my life, and I am going to miss him.

Giving Back

Dad's job was caring for the estate of timber baron Cyrus Yawkey. Consequently, so I could say "inheritance and trust fund" before I could say Eisenhower. Mention of Mr. Yawkey's descendants was so constant you would have thought I didn't have any Forester relatives. Money was our lingua franca.

Dad was equally protective of what he made. My clothes were hand-me-downs from my older brother John that first came from the Montgomery Ward catalog and later from JCPenney. We took one family vacation. He paid me a dime a month if I turned off the lights in empty rooms that month, and he paid me a nickel if he could cut my hair that left me looking like a four-year-old Marine reject.

I couldn't escape money this, money that. That attitude encased me, so I had no concept of poverty. Dad's affair with

Alice made it worse because she had the money, and that skewed everything around her.

I hated being associated with the Yawkey wealth because it set me apart from the kids at school. I was not one of them. I wanted to think I wasn't that different, but I carried the Yawkey wealth tag in a working-class city. I was vastly different.

My first act of philanthropy was age five, telling Grandmother Ethyl Moss Forester, that I wanted to trade my brand-new bright red truck for the battered blue truck she was about to give to the Methodist church rummage sale. A poor boy who had no toys deserved the bright red fire truck more than I did. I do not know where the urge comes from because neither Mom nor Dad ever expressed any interest in using what they had to improve lives in Wausau.

Dad did use Yawkey estate money as the lead gift in a capital campaign to replace the aging YMCA, where I learned how to swim nude with a larger modern facility. He did the same with Yawkey money when he spreadhead the campaign to merge the two hospitals, Memorial and St. Mary's, into a single, modern larger facility with the latest medical technology. He recognized Wausau needed those facilities, but it benefited the Yawkey estate. Those gifts were charitable donations that lowered the taxes the Yawkey estate paid the state and federal government. He was so miserly; I cannot imagine him being philanthropic.

The funny thing about wealthy people, they never have enough. It baffled me when my stepmother, Alice, told me she never sat on the board of the nonprofits she supported. Why the hell did she bother serving on the board if she was not supporting it? Weird logic. Imagine Daddy Warbucks serving on the board of the orphanage and refusing to give them a dime.

I got a clue why she did it; she liked being in control of her money. She gave her grandfather's Greek Revival mansion and carriage house to the Marathon County Historical Society. When the first director did something she disapproved of, she could do nothing about it because she didn't have a seat on the board. That frustrated her because she was used to telling people what they could do, and they did what she said because she was the one holding the purse.

Years later, when she and Dad converted her Wausau home with multiple additions into an art museum, her passive-aggressive constant involvement with the art museum kept the director from ever doing something she disapproved of.

If I had ever told her that, she would have been offended. It's good to be the king.

I don't understand the mindset of billionaire, ultra conservative, queer wingnut Peter Thiel who supports far right politicians and causes when his wealth could do so much good for the community.

Al Baum and Jim Hormel were my model philanthropists. They were smart philanthropists because they stayed current with the non-profits they supported, dining with the executive director and staying in touch with friends on the board. Before they made a gift, they wanted assurances that the organization had the staff it needed, so it had a good chance of being around fifty years later. They were smart investors, and they understood the workings of a nonprofit better more than some nonprofit execs.

I knew the minute I agreed to join the board of the Human Rights Campaign Fund that giving them money was part of the deal. I enrolled in a three-day fundraising workshop at Mills College so I could learn how to raise money. That also made me smarter when I led the founders committee of the Gay and Lesbian Affinity group that raised $3.5 million for the Main Library campaign.

Personal relationships are the heart of fundraising, and one of the most persuasive arguments for raising money for the library was not asking someone for money but asking them to join me in achieving the goal of the library campaign, giving the community its first gay and lesbian center in a public institution.

My success with the library campaign convinced author Katherine V. Forest I could save Lambda Literary Foundation that she had just bailed out. That was the beginning of my involvement with Lambda Literary. After a year on the board, I left because it was dysfunctional. One board member can turn a board dysfunctional, and this one was a doozy. I continued to support Lambda Literary as the board went through changes. Executive Director Tony Valenzuela initiated many of them. His successor, Sue Landers, did a remarkable job saving Lambda Literary when the Covid-19 pandemic shut everything down. Now it functions as a competent nonprofit; the one thing it lacks is a development director.

Nonprofits need more than generous donors and staff who believe in the mission. They need people who know what it takes to keep a nonprofit functioning. Michael Samuel, a budding writer, is a banker with many years at the Federal Reserve Bank. I asked him to join the board of Lambda Literary. Since he joined the board, his financial smarts have been invaluable in keeping the books in order. He also keeps their books meticulously organized, which makes annual budgeting much smoother and more accurate. All parts of a nonprofit's leadership must work in harmony, and that makes them no easier to operate than running a business.

Your everyday person thinks giving away money is a walk in the park, fancy cocktail parties and Cadillacs. The list of fortunes that evaporated due to poor management and bad investments like the Vanderbilt estate is long and storied. At a time when the disparity between the rich and poor is at new heights, I'm afraid to say that for me to be a smart philanthropist, I must respect money for what I can do

With Dad's death, I was able to increase my philanthropy, so I asked Michael Samuel to be my research guy because he knows the right questions to ask, and doing research is his thing. I prefer to make a few substantial gifts than scattering gifts to a multitude of groups. One of my first such gifts was funding a Lambda Literary Award for a writer like me who started writing late in life. I named the award after Michael because he deserves the spotlight. In the first year, ninety-four people applied for the award.

My second, because I have graduate degrees in city planning and poetry, was a scholarship for a queer city planning graduate student at Cal Poly. It is important for the community to know its history, so I named it the Wilfred Owen scholarship. He was the young gay English poet who died in the Great War. I also made donations to Horizons Foundation, the queer Bay Area community foundation, the Sebastopol Senior Center, the only senior center in the state that addresses the needs of the queer community, and queer groups like the Trevor Project.

Giving money to make queer people stronger feels good. It also keeps me connected to the community that has given me so much.

I wrote my first will years before the AIDS epidemic, and I have updated it over the years to match my interests. I set up a charitable remainder trust, CRT, when I sold a building because it gave me a huge tax break. A CRT assures certain groups that they will get something when I take off for the Glorious Bathhouse in the Sky.

One way that a queer person can make their philanthropy greater is by leaving something in their will because when they die there will be more of your money to go around than what you give every year. You are not just making the queer nonprofit stronger because they know they have is a secure future source of income, your legacy lives on long after you die.

I can never fully repay San Francisco and the queer community for all they have given me.

It's been a fantastic ride!

Ω

Rear End

I only get to die once. At some point, my body will reach its due date, and it will shut down.

Death is loss of consciousness.

Dad lived to be ninety-five, my great, great-grandmother in the Quarles family lived to be one hundred and eleven, and I survived HIV forty-two years, so my genes are robust.

I don't know what I'm going to do if the young stud with a short white towel around his waist at the rainbow gate won't let my HIV virus get into the Glorious Bathhouse in the Sky. It served me well, and I will drop it only if the Virus Academy assures me that it will give my virus a medal for Longevity because few HIV viruses have lasted as Long as mine has.

I don't know what spirits consume in the spirit world, but I'm sure when I get there, Michael will have prepared a spirit meal for me using one of his mother's favorite recipes.

My life exceeded my dreams.

About the Author

Chuck Forester was raised in northern Wisconsin and attended Dartmouth and Penn and holds a MCP in city planning and an MFA in poetry. He spent two years in the Peace Corp in Chile with his wife and his son was born shortly after they arrived in San Francisco in 1971. Chuck worked for three San Francisco mayors before serving as an executive with several nonprofits. He was chairman of the Board of the Human Rights Campaign Committee, now the Human Rights Campaign (HRC) and he led the effort that raised $3.5 million for the Hormel Gay and Lesbian Center at the SF Public Library. Since coming out Chuck's has had a keen interest in supporting LGBT literature and preserving LGBT history. Chuck had the good fortune to come out in 1972 in the most supportive possible environment. Michael A. Schoch, his partner of eighteen years, succumbed to AIDS in 1994. Chuck has been living with HIV since 1987. He is the author of *Our Time* and *Eat, Sleep, Love*.

www.ingramcontent.com/pod-product-compliance
Lightning Source LLC
Chambersburg PA
CBHW060527160726
47991CB00001B/215